# Come in the House

## Faith Lessons from Shake Rag and Beyond

Howard Williams

© 2015

Published in the United States by Nurturing Faith Inc., Macon GA,

www.nurturingfaith.net.

Library of Congress Cataloging-in-Publication Data is available.

ISBN 978-1-938514-75-3

All rights reserved. Printed in the United States of America

Scripture quotations are from New Revised Standard Version Bible, copyright © 1989 National Council of the Churches of Christ in the United States of America. Used by permission. All rights reserved.

I put off reading Howard William's journal of life anticipating painful memories of a dear friend and colleague. That was a mistake. There was pain but far more joy. As I read, I felt him whispering in my ear. Fred Craddock wrote that the most powerful communication of the gospel is in whispers. Howard was not a shouter. His soft voice carried truth and feeling. This journal whispers to us as he would tell his story to someone he loved. This work of wisdom and wit brought to mind a favorite spiritual writer and a favorite literary work. The former was Thomas Merton, who said that Jesus had the power to reveal the extraordinary in the ordinary. Howard left that gift in his manuscript. The reader will be moved by memories of their own loved ones. Howard's confessions of stumbles along the path bring smiles to the readers lips as we remember personal missteps.

The other thing that came to mind was Thornton Wilder's classic American play "Our Town." Surely it is the most read and performed American drama. In the play a woman who dies long before she should is permitted to return to earth and home for one day. After being struck by the wonder of people in her life and little ordinary daily events, Emily cries out to her guide: "Does anyone ever realize life while they live it... every, every minute?" Her companion responds " No. Saints and poets maybe..." Howard Williams has left us a diary of the ordinary that puts him in the class of "saints and poets." The reader will be tempted to hurry through the book in a single sitting but it will be most effective in small bites followed by thoughts of one's own journey.

Raymond Bailey

# Foreword

Howard Williams knew how to celebrate the little things in life, and that, more than almost anything else, is the purpose of this book: to remind us to celebrate the little things and to love one another while doing so.

I met Howard one night about ten years ago when he came for visitation to thank us for coming to Weatherly Heights Baptist Church. My daughter, Emma, was a little less than two years old at the time, and my son, Matthew, had just been born. Emma, being a night owl, was still awake but seemed to be wearing her shy PJs that night for once in her life. She was afraid of the big, tall, bald guy who was talking to her mommy and daddy in the living room, so she kept peeking around the wall from the foyer.

Howard smiled at my girl and spoke to her as if she truly mattered.

She's loved him ever since. And so have I.

Howard loved.

About three years ago, Howard wasn't feeling himself, and sometimes, being the frail beings we are, it showed through the ministry he was offering to the church during the opening announcements. But it never interfered with his ability to notice and celebrate the lives that surrounded him. Once, during the middle of his announcements, Matthew, who is on the autism spectrum and doesn't speak often, decided to let out a "YEE-HAW!" at the top of his lungs. The rafters shake when the voiceless speak, and Howard, always listening for a still small voice, certainly heard this one.

My friend stopped, looked at me, and smiled. And he told all of us, "Y'all, I just have to stop for a moment cause I just got a 'Yee-haw!'"

More than almost anyone I've known, Howard knew how to appreciate the little things in life. And that's the legacy he leaves with us here. Whether it was seeing the light of God in some delicious homemade sausage or in the wonder of a child's eyes witnessing the miracle and blessing of birth, Howard saw the little things, the little ones in life. He always invited us to come on in, sit a while, have a bite to eat, and celebrate together the joy and the suffering, the triumph and the pain of this life.

Because it is in the little things that we can best see the handiwork of the God who invites us to come in the house.

Russell Winn<br>
Sunday, March 1, 2015<br>
Huntsville, Alabama

# Contents

Foreword ..................................................................... v

Come in the House ................................................... 1
Communion ............................................................... 3
The Resurrection of Daddy Freeman ..................... 5
Lost ............................................................................... 7
Upside Down .............................................................. 9
I'll Fly Away .............................................................. 11
Touch .......................................................................... 13
Today They Wore Green ........................................ 15
Till Death Do Us Part ............................................. 16
Things I Learned from My Dad ............................ 18
Pregnant? ................................................................... 20
The Taste of Florsheim ........................................... 21
The Sermon ............................................................... 23
The Pocketknife ....................................................... 25
The Gift ...................................................................... 27
The Fight ................................................................... 28
The Devil Made Me Do It ..................................... 30
The Camera ............................................................... 32
The Big Dance .......................................................... 34
The Bad and the Good ........................................... 36
Sunday School Sweats ............................................ 38
Snakes and Gardens ................................................ 40
Scars ........................................................................... 42
Possum ....................................................................... 44

| | |
|---|---:|
| Party Line | 46 |
| Ol' Mike | 48 |
| Luggage | 50 |
| Loretta | 52 |
| Looking Back | 54 |
| Learning to Drive | 56 |
| Leaning | 58 |
| Valentines | 60 |
| Quirky Kid | 62 |
| Phone Call from God | 64 |
| It Was a Miracle | 66 |
| I Hear That Train a-Rollin' | 68 |
| I Hate | 70 |
| House Fire | 72 |
| Here, Chick, Chick | 74 |
| Hammer Time | 76 |
| Green Grass | 78 |
| God's Cheers | 79 |
| Hell's Fire | 80 |
| Fire Ants | 82 |
| Elliott and Lonnie | 84 |
| Eggs to Ashes | 86 |
| Deliver Me from Evil | 88 |
| Bogue Creek | 90 |
| Belonging | 92 |
| Balancing…Life | 94 |
| A Wild Rose | 95 |
| Water Haul | 97 |
| Turkeys and Thanksgiving | 99 |

| | |
|---|---|
| Beagles | 101 |
| Christmas Sounds | 103 |
| Christmas Laughter | 104 |
| The Mansion | 106 |
| Billy's Grand Adventure | 108 |
| It Was a Miracle, Too | 110 |
| Epilogue | 112 |

# Come in the House

The long gravel driveway that came off the main road down to my grandmother's house in Shake Rag gave ample opportunity to get ready to greet visitors. The windows and doors were always open in the summer because even though they had a window air conditioner, they never turned it on except when *As the World Turns* came on around midday. Through those open doors you could hear the rumble of the pickup truck and see the plume of dust trailing, so you always knew when company was coming. Sometimes on Sundays Mama Bea would pray before issuing the invitation. She would look out, see the familiar truck, and say, "Lord, here comes Billy Brown!" with just a bit of disgust in her voice. Then came the bang of the screen door as it was flung open and the same hearty greeting from Mama Bea that everyone received, "Come in the house."

Billy was a TV repairman with one arm who was strong enough to lift TVs that normally required two grown men. He was born and reared in Shake Rag. He always had the same coveralls on and always smelled musty. Billy had a loud voice with a bit of a rasp that carried easily through the four-room, cinder-block house. It was well known in our family that Billy was smitten with my older sister, who was twenty years his junior. That little bit of information was great fodder for this younger brother's teasings. Such thoughts seem strange by today's standards, but I guess thirty-five years ago in Mississippi, it wasn't that uncommon. I need to add that my sister never returned his affections.

Billy would visit for most of the afternoon, lingering until the *Wonderful World of Disney* came on and it was time for supper. Then the cloth that covered the table and Sunday dinner came off to reveal the remains of roast beef, fried chicken, an occasional rabbit or squirrel, green beans, boiled okra, squash, cornbread, butterbeans, peas, chocolate pie and coconut cake, not to mention the potato salad with mayonnaise that we thought was as fresh as it had been five hours earlier. After the unveiling we all got a little quiet, except for the rattling of silverware and iced tea glasses. The second feast was always as good as the first. Then Billy Brown would leave with a big smile, a full stomach, and a thank you. "Better get on home, Bea," he would say as he clamored into his truck. Mama Bea would stand on the porch and watch until the plume of dust had settled on the cotton plants, and then she came in. There was no doubt that Billy Brown was a little different from most, even a bit strange and unsettling, but except for that hushed prayer, you would never know it by the way he was treated at Mama Bea's.

As soon as Billy Brown crossed over that threshold, he was received and accepted as he was. There were no expectations for change. He was Billy Brown, a guest. That was enough.

Billy Brown is buried in the back right corner of Boone's Chapel Cemetery there in Shake Rag. It's a good place as cemetery plots go. Just a few over are Mama Bea and Daddy Freeman and a host of other relatives. I wouldn't mind being buried there myself. It feels like home. One day there will be a door flung open wide, and our Lord will welcome us all home. There will be no distinction, and the tablecloth will be pulled back to reveal a banquet of plenty. We'll all be treated as what we are: sons and daughters, brothers and sisters. That will be enough.

# Communion

Celtic Christians were people of the land — agrarian people — but their connection to the land was more than economic. For them the land on which they lived was sacred. It was as if they were inextricably bound to it. It was the place of family, and it was a gift from their Creator. I have places like that for me. Shake Rag, Mississippi, is one of them. Every few years I go back to the place where my mother was raised and reminisce about a few acres that I was allowed to roam freely with a single shot shotgun and an old dog named Mike. We took on many dragons and slew them all.

Up the road is Boone's Chapel Methodist Church. It is the first place that I had a real conversation with God. The story is a bit long, but around the age of ten, I became keenly aware that there was a Someone who loved me. Out behind the church is the cemetery. There are over 300 folks buried there, and I think I might be related to almost all of them. A couple years ago I walked the grounds of the cemetery, remembering my grandparents, my aunts and uncles, a cousin who died too soon, and a local TV repairman who often dropped by for Sunday dinner at Mama Bea's. There were also tables, long tables that stretched out along the side of the church forever. I remember community gatherings on those tables that I know are older than even my memories of them. Fried chicken, green beans, tomatoes, coconut cakes, fried corn, and giant jars of tea filled every available space. I have to wonder if those tables are still being filled or if all the saints who once gathered around the tables have now taken up residence behind the church. Has the community that once broke bread on rough-hewn planks now gathered to celebrate Communion at the banquet table with our Lord?

Among those was Daddy Freeman, my grandfather. I only knew Daddy Freeman as a farmer. But before that, during the Depression, he ran a little country store in Shake Rag that was big enough to meet the basic needs of that small rural community. As you know, the Depression was a dark time in the history of this country, and Shake Rag wasn't immune to its effects. People were hungry — even people who lived on farms and could raise most of their food. Growing food in the summer, though, is of little value in the winter if you can't afford the jars to preserve it. So Daddy Freeman sold on credit — a little here, a little there — knowing full well that every two bits of supplies that walked out the door would never be repaid. That was okay, though, because people were hungry, and that's what a community does. It shares the burden.

That day, as I walked and felt the sacredness of the land beneath my feet, I was reminded of that "great cloud of witnesses" that Paul speaks of in Hebrews. They witnessed years ago to a skinny ten-year-old about a mystery, about fellowship, simple faith, and the importance of community. They witnessed to the next generation about faith and about Communion, not from little glass cups and bits of crackers while sitting on well-polished pews, but from big jars of tea and cornbread around long tables. It was true communion, gifts of God for the people of God…southern style.

# The Resurrection of Daddy Freeman

By the time I came to know my grandfather, Daddy Freeman, he had made some significant changes in his life, one of which, I am told, is that he had quit drinking. It seems that in his younger days he had a bit of a wild streak in him. This wild streak led him on binges that might keep him out all night or longer with his buddies. Mama Bea was a worrier, and she would sit up waiting for him to find his way home, even if it meant waiting all night. One particular weekend Daddy Freeman had been gone a little bit longer than usual, and Mama Bea was almost beside herself. Then she heard the rumble of a car coming down the gravel drive. The distance from their house and the main road was probably about 150 yards, so as soon as she heard the car, she had plenty of time to get outside and prepare herself for a proper reception of her wayward husband.

This time was different, though. Instead of the snarling and flying frying pans, Mama Bea took one look and began wailing at the top of her lungs. Great tears were flowing as she saw one of Daddy Freeman's friends coming down the driveway. It was Mr. Smith. "Ohhhh, Baby!" she said to her son. "It's finally happened. Here comes Mr. Smith bringing your daddy home." Now, it wasn't unusual for a friend to bring Daddy Freeman home, but Mr. Smith is not the one you wanted to see. Mr. Smith, as it turns out, was the Chickasaw County funeral home director, and he was bringing Daddy Freeman home in the hearse! Mama Bea thought Daddy Freeman was dead, and I'm certain that if Daddy Freeman had been sober enough to see Mama Bea, he probably was wishing that he was. In fact, I think I might have climbed in the back and reclined until the storm was over, Jesus had come back, or I had succumbed to natural causes. "FREEMAN!" no doubt reverberated all over Shake Rag that day.

I don't know what happened following the one and only resurrection of Daddy Freeman. Maybe that is when he decided to quit drinking. Maybe Mama Bea knocked a knot on his head and encouraged him along the road to sobriety. Knowing my mischievous grandfather, he probably got a good laugh out of it in a day or two.

"Lazarus, come out," Jesus said. And he did. Not from the back of a party wagon called a hearse but from a tomb. What a joyous day! Hearing his name called and then being greeted by Jesus and Mary and Martha and the others must have been, well, a miraculous feeling. One day Jesus will call our name.

Howard, come out. Ruth, come out. Bill, come out. We will be raised, reunited, and resurrected.

What about the meantime? What about now? Wait. Listen. Don't you hear it? Every day? Howard. Ruth. Bill. Come out! Leave behind the bindings, the tomb of addiction, the darkness of depression. Come out, all of you, to be resurrected to the newness of life in Christ! We can live because he lives. So let's go out and live it up, the way God intended.

And the people said, "Amen."

# Lost

As a young boy I loved tromping around the farm in Shake Rag. Mama Bea and Daddy Freeman's place was right in the middle of my uncles' farms. On one side there was a strip of land that Daddy Freeman rented from his brother, William Ogg. On the other side was the farmland that was owned by Mama Bea's brother, Charlie Sullivan. The bottom was bordered by another of Mama Bea's brothers, Earl.

I knew each parcel as well as I knew my quarter acre of backyard where I grew up in Grenada, Mississippi. I knew each pond and where the best fishing spot was on each of the ponds. The covey of quail could always be found along a ridge down across the bottom on Uncle William's side of the fence, right by the hayfield. Red Bud Creek separated two of the farms and was quite the formidable foe when my little legs tried to climb its steep banks. My Uncle Fred found a confederate cannon ball in Red Bud Creek when he was a boy. A much smaller creek fed Red Bud and flowed up alongside Daddy Freeman's place. For some time it served as the dumping ground for tin cans and other such things that couldn't be burned or eaten by the chickens and hogs. There was a grove of oak trees on Daddy Freeman's place that served as a sanctuary for family reunions in the summers.

One day my cousin Gary and I decided to make our usual rounds through the Sullivan/Ogg kingdoms. We left the house with our usual weapons of choice. My options were a single shot .22 rifle or a single shot 20-gauge shotgun. The shotgun was my favorite and was my choice for this day of adventure. We meandered across pastures and through woods, kicking briar patches along the way, watching for the familiar white flag of the cottontail rabbit as it would jump and run. We were gone for hours. In all our traipsing about, somehow we got disoriented. Suddenly the markers that we relied on to identify our location were gone. Everything became very unfamiliar, and we began to understand how Dorothy and her companions felt in the forest on their journey to Oz. The trees certainly were watching us, and I was quite certain a branch had grabbed at me.

We were both about to cry, though neither of us would ever admit it, when we came to a very steep hill. We decided to make the climb. Maybe we could see something familiar and make our way home. Home. That's where we wanted to be in the worst way. So we climbed. As we clamored to the top, we discovered that the hill was just a pond bank. We peered out across the water with disappointment and ever-increasing fear. Never mind that we had discovered a new body of water and that Lewis and Clark had nothing on us. We wanted to be home. Then we lifted our eyes up from the water to see what was ahead. Unbelievable. There was Mama Bea's house just 200 yards away. We were actually standing on the very banks of their pond, the pond that I had fished and wandered around since I could walk. Our fear had blinded us to the familiar. Our meandering had not carried us away to some far-off country. In fact, we had never really left home at all.

Home. Being home. That is grace. We lose our way, wandering about, feeling lost, helpless, fearful. Never recognizing the many signs along the way that direct us back, beckoning, whispering our name, calling us home. Then, one day, it all becomes clear. The God who created us, called us by name, and loves us had never left us, nor did we or could we ever leave God's ever-gracious presence. We had been home all along. We've but to recognize it, believe it, receive it, and live into it. Grace abounds.

> *For I am convinced that neither death, nor life, nor angels, nor rulers, nor things present, nor things to come, nor powers, nor height, nor depth, nor anything else in all creation, will be able to separate us from the love of God in Christ Jesus our Lord.* — Romans 8:38-39

# Upside Down

Growing up in Shake Rag would have been better than Disney World for little boys. Hunting, fishing, and meandering through the woods and creek would have offered a plethora of imaginative adventures. However, if you were a high-spirited, pretty girl, things may have been a little slow. That was my mom. At least that is how I picture her. She was always a bit mischievous with me growing up. She once took great delight in wrapping a book for Christmas by putting a rattle inside. It drove me nuts for about three weeks trying to guess what was inside. She got that devilishness from Daddy Freeman.

Anyway, Mom, or Sista as she was called growing up, probably helped Mama Bea with the house, caught chickens for Sunday dinner, fished a bit, and played on the hay bales in the barn, among other things. That's all fine when you are ten or twelve. But when those teen years hit, this farmer's daughter had other ideas about fun. Specifically, this Baptist girl liked to dance.

One Saturday night there was going to be a dance in the barn at Uncle Earl's or somewhere nearby. She asked Daddy Freeman about going, and he responded with a firm "NO!" Well, he might as well have said yes because this high-spirited, mischievous, Baptist farmer's daughter was going to the dance with or without Daddy Freeman's approval. To get to Uncle Earl's, you had to go across the bottom (a low-lying area of pasture for you city folk), cross Red Bud Creek (there wasn't a bridge), get through several barbed-wire gaps (gates), and travel through a cottonfield or two. That was no step for a stepper, though. Sista decided to wait until it was night, and she would saddle up the old mule and head out under the cover of darkness. So she did. I can just hear the old screen door creaking as she gently opens and closes the door on her way out to the barn. The old dog lying in the cool dust opens one eye then shuts it as if he's seen this before. Watching for the dangers that are inherent around cows and barnyards, she carefully stepped her way out, threw the saddle on the mule, and took off for the dance.

Sista knew how to ride, and the old mule knew how to run, so things were going pretty good at first. Then she noticed the saddle was a bit askew. She wrestled it back up. Then it slid a bit further to the side. It seems that Sista had forgotten to cinch the saddle properly in her haste, and she was about to be on a ride that even Disney couldn't match. Down across the bottom she went when all of a sudden, the saddle flipped and the world was suddenly upside down.

Stars were where the ground should have been, and she certainly shouldn't be seeing mule hooves flipping up past her nose.

About this time in the retelling of this story, Mom was always laughing so hard she never finished it. How she got the mule to stop will forever be a mystery. Whether she made it to the dance or not is unknown, although I suspect she did. And I'm quite certain she paid a hefty price when she got home. I'm equally certain that was not the last time she sneaked off to the dance.

"Upside down" is probably what the rich young ruler thought of Jesus' comments, "Sell all you have and give it to the poor." "Upside down" is probably what the disciples thought as the woman poured the expensive perfume on Jesus' feet. "Upside down" is probably what the crowd thought when Lazarus came stumbling out of the tomb.

Spend some time with Jesus, and that's what life becomes, "upside down." That poor person won't blend into the concrete, and you'll wonder how you can help. The poverty of forsaken places like Calcutta will become rich with opportunities to share God's grace. Homeless children will become your children. Injustice, greed, abusive power, inhospitableness, fractured relationships, and a myriad of other common ingredients in our world will begin to stare down at you like giant billboards. This week, today even, see the people around you. Don't stare through them; really take a long look and see if maybe you can do something to help cinch their saddles, make their world more "right," more just, more peaceful, more the way Jesus intended.

Giddy up!

## I'll Fly Away

I have a favorite uncle on my mother's side. Actually, he's my only uncle on my mother's side, but if he weren't, he would be. I'll call him "Uncle Fred." Uncle Fred grew up at Shake Rag and is the source of many of my stories that occurred before I was even conceived, I mean, thought about. He is a veteran of the Korean War and then served the state of Mississippi as a highway patrolman. He served faithfully for a hundred years or so, eventually becoming district supervisor. After retiring he had a brief stint as sheriff in his small town in north Mississippi. I always said he could have been on a recruiting poster. He is tall and has a stare that could stop most crooks in their tracks. I have a vivid memory of him pulling my mother and me over on I-55 as we made our way home from Memphis. As we stood on the side of the road chatting, my mother took her empty Coke bottle and heaved it out away from the highway. With arms folded, dark glasses, and wide-brimmed hat on, Uncle Fred stared down at her and said in a low but stern voice, "Sista, that's a $500 fine."

With his military and law enforcement career, it's no wonder that folks would naturally turn to him when disaster strikes. There is one lady in particular that calls Uncle Fred even when the tiniest of clouds comes floating by. Now, Uncle Fred is a good man, a deacon of First Baptist Church and long on patience. However, Uncle Fred finally ran out of that patience, and the next phone call he got from the dear lady concerning some benign thunder cloud brought this response: "Mrs. Smith, why don't you just put a cell phone in your pocket, and when you land, call me. I'll come get you."

Dorothy could have used that advice when she landed in Oz. That is, if cell phones had been invented. "Auntie Em? This is Dorothy. Are you ok? That was some twister. Yes, I'm fine. The house isn't quite the same. As a matter of fact, nothing is quite the same. There was this witch, and there are little people, and everything is in color, and, well, I don't know how to get home. Could you come get me?"

Or Elijah, you know, the prophet who was taken away by the whirlwind. Elijah: "Dude, I'm ridin' this whirlwind, and we just passed over Kilimanjaro. Oops, clipped a pink flamingo." Then there's Enoch. Who knows what happened to him? "I was there, now I'm not."

One day, we will be here, and then not. Jesus said he has prepared a place for us. What if we could have cell phones? "This isn't quite what I expected, but you know, I like it. You won't believe who I just saw. That grace thing was way bigger than I ever imagined. No, don't be in any hurry about getting here. There's plenty more to do where you are. Things are so clear now. Love. Peace. Grace. Tell Auntie Em not to worry. I'm home."

Why don't you join with me in singing or humming "I'll Fly Away"? It seems appropriate. But before you do, put a cell phone in your pocket. You just never know.

# Touch

An old friend crossed my path this week. It was a friend who shares many of the same circles of friends as I, but it just seems that we never circle at the same time. Let's call him James. James and I were chatting about life in general when I asked about how he was staying busy in retirement. The response included things about family, a Sunday school class, and volunteering at a local shelter that feeds the homeless. I could see passion as he began to share some of the things he was doing there. Then he told me of a recent experience. James said he had just finished passing out bologna sandwiches to the folks who had gathered. He left the building feeling quite good about himself and the ministry when he looked over to see one of the families sitting in their car. They were eating their dry bologna sandwiches. Can you picture it in your imagination? It surely must have been a very sad sight. James remembered the family. He had served them the sandwiches. He remembered looking them in the eye as they passed by. Then it dawned on him. He had not touched them. Handing the sandwiches, smelling their odor, he had passed them on down the line and out the door without a touch. He wondered if anyone had touched them that day or even that week. James said, "I thought that I had been Jesus to someone that day. What I realized was that I hadn't been Jesus to anyone. Not a one."

In 1979 AT&T, facing a growing public distrust due to its potential monopoly, developed a very successful ad campaign. The campaign's slogan was "Reach out and touch someone." Even AT&T recognized the value of touch and tried to capture that value for their bottom line.

Jesus often healed with just a touch. He recognized that touch has a healing quality in and of itself. When I go visit those in the hospital or the nursing home, I am always careful to touch the person I'm visiting. Occasionally it is not appropriate, but more often than not, a gentle touch is appreciated.

Touch also breaks down barriers. Barriers of culture, religion, generational differences, disagreement, and others can be dissolved with a simple touch of the hand. It communicates openness, equality, and value. This was demonstrated to me quite poignantly with another friend. There had been a disagreement. I worried that perhaps the disagreement had been of such magnitude that reconciliation would be long and hard. That is, until Sunday rolled around and I felt a gentle pat on my back. I turned to see my friend walking past. The walls of disagreement could be heard crumbling and falling to the floor, all because of a touch. Touch is important. Touch is healing. Touch restores.

James didn't touch that family that day. But James was touched by Jesus, I think. James may not have been Jesus that day at the shelter, but he certainly became more like Jesus as he received a touch, a nudge, a reminder from the Spirit that we all need to be touched…and that we all need to reach out and touch someone, sometime, in Jesus' name.

*Jesus stretched out his hand and touched him…* — Mark 1:41

## Today They Wore Green

As we pulled into the Grissom High School parking lot, I reminded Abigail about the tragedy that had occurred over the weekend. Hogan Vaughn, a senior at Grissom, was killed in a single car accident. It is another tragedy that hits the school that still grieves over the deaths of Leigh Anna and Tad, killed by a drunk driver. Abigail's response to my reminder was, "I know, Dad; that's why I'm wearing green." I looked over and saw the bright green shirt that she had put on this morning. It had gone unnoticed by me until now. Then I looked around campus, and at the same time Abigail said, "See." Every student was wearing green, every single one — dark green, bright green, light green, khaki green, camouflage green. Through the miracle of texting, word had gone out to honor Hogan and, I think, to grieve together yet another loss. I fabricated a cough as I told Abigail goodbye in hopes of disguising the emotion that was quickly rising to the surface. It was a moment of sorrow and gratitude, realizing that these "kids" had to endure such pain so young, but at the same time, they "get it."

That day at Grissom, there weren't any football players, band members, club members, nerds, minorities, internationals, skaters, Goths, or anyone or anything else that divides and stratifies. They were only green. The color we identify with envy, that day was the color of compassion, of solidarity, and of love. The students at Grissom remind us that what is important doesn't divide us but unites us.

It is a lesson that is easily learned but hardly lived. Finding fault is much easier. Dwelling on our differences is often preferred. Pointing fingers at another is more comfortable than embracing the other. Listening is too difficult.

We are part of one another, gathered and united by God's spirit. When one suffers, we all suffer. Let us all work to build up the body, encourage the body, love the body. Let God's spirit work so that we produce compassion, humility, and the ability to celebrate one another.

Today I wore blue. I think tomorrow I'll wear green. How about you?

*As it is, there are many members, yet one body.... If one member suffers, all suffer together with it.* — 1 Corinthians 12:20, 26

*By this everyone will know that you are my disciples, if you have love for one another.* — John 13:35

# Till Death Do Us Part

My daughter has been dating a wonderful young man for about a year now. It wasn't very long after they began dating that we discovered that we are related. Being from Mississippi, that didn't come as much of a shock, especially since it was from my Shake Rag side of the family. It turned out that his great-great Aunt Hortense was married to my great Uncle Earl. It's a small world, I guess, at least in Mississippi.

We began talking about this in the family circle, and a story surfaced that I had never heard before. It turns out that Uncle Earl had been married twice. His first wife had died, and he married Aunt Hortense, the only aunt of the two that I ever knew. Now, Uncle Earl was a practical man, so when his first wife died, he bought a double plot in the cemetery at Boone's Chapel Methodist Church in Shake Rag. Boone's Chapel Cemetery is where all my relatives are buried, going back to the 1800s. You can't step over a grave without stepping over a cousin or aunt or uncle. My grandparents are there, along with others who weren't relatives but probably thought they were. So when Uncle Earl went on to his reward, it was only natural that he would be buried beside his first wife. In fact, it was his request, being the practical man that he was.

Practical or not, Aunt Hortense was livid. She had given him the best years of her life, and she should be the wife that Uncle Earl found his eternal home next to. Aunt Hortense just couldn't let it rest, so to speak. So she went and found a grader blade — a long steel blade you see on road graders that is used to smooth road foundations. They seem to be about six feet long and about three feet tall. I can't imagine how much it must weigh. Aunt Hortense wrestled that huge piece of flat steel up to the Boone's Chapel Cemetery, along with a sledgehammer. She took the blade and put it between Uncle Earl and his first wife and began pounding. She beat that thing until it served as a suitable divide between him and "her." Forever.

I'm sure Aunt Hortense was a good Baptist, as was most of my Shake Rag family. She would have known about the gospel story where Jesus is quizzed by the Sadducees, who were trying to catch him in a misstep. They want to trap Jesus by basically asking if we will have more than one spouse in heaven if we had more than one on earth. Jesus' response was that it wasn't important.

Now, I like to think that Jana will be waiting on me in heaven one day or that I'll be waiting on her. I want to think that the relationship will truly be beyond "till death do us part." But I can't count on it. What I can count on is that we will all be joyfully received into the kingdom, into the loving Creator's arms, surrounded by the Spirit, and greeted by the living Christ. There we will live, truly live, and we will love like we have never loved or been loved before. That, I can count on. Grader blades or not.

Forever.

# Things I Learned from My Dad

1. How to tie a fisherman's knot. A simple thing to teach but so very important. Not to just catch fish, but to tell a son, "I have time for you."

2. Don't panic when things go wrong. We once had a flat returning from hunting quail when I was about ten years old. It was dark, and we had to let the dogs out of the trunk to get to the spare. Off they went, running through the dark woods, out into the highway, all over the place. I began to cry, afraid for the dogs and afraid for us. Dad calmly fixed the flat, reassured me, called the dogs back to the car, and we headed home.

3. Some things are best left for professionals. Dad grew up with the belief that he could fix anything. He was most fond of tinkering around the back of our old black and white TV. That was back when the closest thing to electronics in TVs were those old glass tubes. He would take the back off the set, find the tube that didn't light up, and replace it. He eventually upgraded to color and then again to a really nice set from Sears, a Magnavox, I think. It quit working one day, so he headed to the back of the set with screwdriver in hand. After hearing a loud pop, I turned to see Dad surrounded in a cloud of smoke. He called a repairman from then on.

4. Not all junk is junk. I have mentioned the attic of our house in the story titled "The Camera." Once in high school I asked Dad if he would like the attic cleaned out. He was agreeable. So up the stairs I went. I quickly decided the fastest way to get rid of the junk was to just toss it out the second-floor window. After working and tossing for about three hours, I looked out to the ground to admire my progress. I looked just in time to see Dad hauling a big armful back into the house. There was barely anything on the ground. He took almost everything right back up the stairs, including saving the camera that had pictures of Mom locked away for thirty years.

5. Listen to experience. After trying unsuccessfully to have children, an attorney came along with the offer of an adoptable newborn, for a fee, of course. I called Dad, explained all the details, and then asked for a loan, a very large loan. Dad knew the importance of what was happening for us but was also uneasy. He said, "Something doesn't sound right." I should have listened. It wasn't "right," and after losing the money and seeing two crooked attorneys go to jail, I recalled his single comment and his desire to see his children happy, despite his uneasiness.

6. Every generation has to touch the oven. See #5.

7. Hedge your bets. When I was a junior in college, I finally decided what I wanted to do with my life professionally. I had been aiming at an accounting degree to be followed by law school. It never seemed to feel right, and while at home one Christmas for break, I told Dad I wanted to go to seminary. He immediately knew what that meant — no rich son to take care of him in his old age! He didn't say that, though. His only comment was, "Well, at least you'll have an accounting degree to fall back on." I waited till later to tell him I was dropping out of accounting too.

8. Marriage is a partnership. Dad didn't teach me this by example. He was quite the opposite. In particular, Dad maintained a tight fist on the money. For a long while he even did the grocery shopping, not wanting Mom to have access to the checkbook. That ended, and he eventually let Mom have that chore. When I was in high school, I wanted a new bike. Mom took me to Memphis, where I picked out a new ten-speed. At the checkout Mom pulled out a wad of bills as big as a baseball, peeled off five twenties, and paid for the bike. She looked at me and said, "Don't you dare tell your dad." Mom had been adding twenty dollars to the grocery bill each week for years. Mom had made partner, and Dad didn't know it!

9. Be a world citizen. The Memphis newspaper (*The Commercial Appeal*) and Walter Cronkite were mainstays in our house. Dad read the newspaper from front to back, every day. I don't think Dad missed Walter a single time in all those years he brought the world into our living room. Dad wanted to know — and it was important to know — what was happening beyond Grenada, Mississippi.

10. Perfection is not a prerequisite to being a dad. Dad had his flaws; he had many flaws actually. But never — not a single time — did I ever question his love and loyalty to me. His "loans," letters, weekly phone calls, birthday surprises, hugs, tuition checks, encouragement, patience, Rebel updates, crappie suppers, love for my wife and children, spanking (only one time), stern looks, big smiles, goofy dances, trust, all of it, were gifts from an imperfect but loving father. I hope to pass that part of him along to my children.

# Pregnant?

Jana and I are pregnant, sort of. Sometime in the next three months we will have a forty-pound bouncing baby boy. Last week we signed papers with the Department of Human Services that commit us to adopting Zackary, our seven-year-old foster son. Zackary has been with us for about three years now.

Zackary's arrival into our lives sounds much like the old tale of the stork making an unexpected delivery. One day while I was on retreat in North Carolina, Jana received a call from a friend of a friend. She asked if we would be interested in adopting Zackary. Jana called me immediately and asked me the question. In about a nanosecond I said yes, so she called the "stork" back. They agreed to meet at the YMCA for a "get to know you" meeting. An hour later, Zackary was in our home for an afternoon visit. Then it was decided he would spend the night. The next day, clothes and toys were delivered, and I arrived home after a dash through three states to find a doe-eyed little boy staring up the length of my 6' 5" frame. We were both scared. That was the beginning of a story that has no end.

Jana and I are not new to adoptions. Abigail was adopted in an equally miraculous turn of events that started as a phone call from a complete stranger. That's another story for another day. The point is that adoption is part of the fabric of our family. We speak of it as easily as others do about their trips to the maternity ward. Both of our children know the path God used to bring them into our lives and us into theirs. We are not blind to the fact that it has been troublesome at times and probably will be yet. But there is also much to celebrate. Being chosen by another is a gift. It says this is no accident; there is intention in our action. We love you; we chose you.

God has done the same for us, chosen us, that is. God through Christ has reached out and embraced us, making us God's daughters and sons with all the benefits and privileges that being God's child means. We become full heirs, receiving all the love, all the grace, all the forgiveness, all of God. That is more than heartwarming; it is soul stirring. What a promise! What a privilege! What a Savior!

Thanks be to God.

*You have received a spirit of adoption. When we cry, "Abba! Father!" it is that very Spirit bearing witness with our spirit that we are children of God.*
— Romans 8:15-16

# The Taste of Florsheim

"What have you said?" was the first thing I heard when I picked up the phone last Monday afternoon. Before I could even think to ask what was on her mind, I knew it didn't matter. I had the sweet taste of shoe leather in my mouth, and my next move would determine where I would sleep that night. Apparently, some of the good folks who read my column each week had not actually read my column last week. They read the teaser, "Jana and I are pregnant," and started shooting her congratulatory emails and questions about due dates and such. Oops!

Unfortunately, that wasn't the first time I had found my Florsheims happily nestled amongst my molars. It seems I have the uncanny ability of saying the wrong thing, always at the wrong time. I've never meant to be mean-spirited; most often I was just dumb. I've congratulated when regrets were in order. I've yammered on when silence was best. I've spoken critically of someone only to find out later I had been talking to their mama. I once preached on about a particular denomination's ridiculous rules regarding music only to find out I was in the midst of a whole covey of them. Oops!

It often feels like I'm the only one gifted in such things. I've never seen others' faces turn to the warm autumn glow of red that mine so frequently does. Perhaps others are able to hide it or disguise their faux pas better than I. Maybe others don't write about their verbal miscues and mistakes for the whole world to read. Maybe.

The writer of James seems to think the malady is more prevalent. James says, "For all of us make many mistakes." He's right. Our missteps with our tongues are a serious problem. It would be good if they only resulted in embarrassing moments. Unfortunately, they often result in real hurt, my own words included. We are quick to chastise, to demean, and to defend ourselves with darts of well-chosen words aimed at another's heart. We betray our friends and our family with linguistic arrows that are shot much too quickly without regard for the damage. Sometimes it offers us a chance to win an argument. Other times it just makes us feel "bigger." Even the rhetoric in our nation today is completely out of control.

How about this week we all dial it back just a little bit? Let our words be encouraging, thoughtful, and responsible. Let's all find ways to affirm our families, our friends, and the clerk in the store. We all make mistakes, maybe every day, but we can do better. How about it?

*For all of us make many mistakes. Anyone who makes no mistakes in speaking is perfect, able to keep the whole body in check with a bridle. If we put bits into the mouths of horses to make them obey us, we guide their whole bodies. Or look at ships: though they are so large that it takes strong winds to drive them, yet they are guided by a very small rudder wherever the will of the pilot directs. So also the tongue is a small member, yet it boasts of great exploits. How great a forest is set ablaze by a small fire! And the tongue is a fire.* — James 3:2-6

# The Sermon

There were two churches in Shake Rag, a Methodist church and a Baptist church. You already know Boone's Chapel Methodist Church. It's where my family and most of Shake Rag's citizens are buried. It's where the community meals were held on the long tables, and it's where I had an up-close encounter with my eternal future in a children's Sunday school class.

The other church, Mount Olive Baptist Church, was just down the road, sort of. Mount Olive is the church where most of my family were members. Actually, I'm not really certain that they were actually members, but I like to think they were. As I recall, it was my Uncle Guinea, or Eugene, or Clyde that built Mount Olive. I don't really know why I think that; it just seems right. It was at Mount Olive as a very young youth that I found out that preachers' kids were often less than angelic when the preacher's son invited me out to the back of the church to smoke a cigarette. I respectfully declined, and I kept an eye on him the rest of the day. The following summer when I returned, the preacher and his less than angelic son had moved.

It was also at Mount Olive that I preached one of my first sermons. It was a big occasion. The church was full with close to forty, maybe fifty in attendance. Almost every one of them was a cousin or an aunt or something in the family tree. It was also the only time I ever saw my grandparents and my parents in church together. In a couple years my mom would die of cancer, and not far behind her my grandmother died.

One of my cousins was the pianist. I don't know how she managed it, but when she played, she touched every key on the board. "Amazing Grace" seemed strangely like a cross between a polka and a rendition by Liberace. Another cousin was the music director. On that particular Sunday he didn't show up. My cousin the pianist said I would have to lead the music. I informed her that I didn't read music and that unless there was a shower around somewhere, she wouldn't be hearing me sing either. She countered my hesitancy: "Just move your hand up in the air when I nod. They'll do the rest." I felt like I had just gotten trumped in a game of spades. I agreed. She went to the piano. I went to the pulpit. She began playing. Even though the hymn was in the book, I didn't recognize what she was playing and didn't have a clue as to where she was. I watched nervously and was beginning to feel a twitch in my right eye when she nodded. Up shot my hand,

and she was right. The good people of Mount Olive began singing and didn't stop until the end. They even knew to skip the third verse.

We did that a couple more times, took up an offering, and then it was my turn to preach. My text was Jonah, the whole book! I don't remember much about the sermon. I suspect there were some points on repentance, something about obedience, and then probably a nod to the idea of forgiveness. At some point the fish in the book was likened in size to some of Daddy Freeman's bass in his pond. He chuckled at the analogy, and it made me happy that he liked it. Nobody got saved that day, except for my cousin the music director, whose absence the rest of the day probably saved him a good chewing out. My dad did say that it had never occurred to him that sermons could be preached more than once (I only had one sermon). He was pleased that I would be paid twice for the same amount of work. Seems to be a common view among many in the pew, not just dad's. On that day, hands were shaken, pats on the back offered, and the preacher boy was sent home feeling the family had blessed him and his calling.

God did that. God looked at his Son and said, "This Son that I love, I am very proud." Or at least God said something like that. We all need that blessing. Each of us longs for a dad or mom or grandparent or teacher to give us their blessing: a word, a pat on the back, an acknowledgment. We need to know that we have worth and that those we love and admire see something of value in us.

God did that too. God looked at us, looks at us, each of us, every day, and says, "This daughter, this son that I love, I am very proud." The notions that we harbor in the recesses of our memories that we are not good enough, that we can do nothing right, the shame that lingers, all that God sets aside, looks at his creation, and declares it "good." What a wonderful gift here in Advent. The child is proof of that love. Receive it. Live into it. Do something today to show that you have received the gift. Call a son or daughter. Pull a student over close. Tell them they are good and that you are very proud. God will be proud you did, all over again.

# The Pocketknife

Any working farm and farmer has a set of tools and equipment that are just standard. A farm has to have a good tractor and a bush hog (giant lawnmower), along with a host of other "attachments" like spreaders and such. A farm has to have buckets and shovels and hoes and axes and barbed wire and lots more stuff. Back in the day, every farm had a hay hook. It was shaped like the letter "J" turned sideways and allowed the user to lift a bale of hay. Today they use forklifts to move hay. A good cotton scale was used on many farms along with the trailer the cotton was piled into from giant sacks. Today they use machines to pick and weigh the cotton.

The farmer usually had a favorite hammer that could nail as well as stretch the barbed wire. Daddy Freeman, you will recall, used his hammer as an encourager for stubborn tillers. He also had a pocketknife. I don't think there was a day that went by that Daddy Freeman didn't have his pocketknife. It was something I marveled at. The blades were sharp and slender, mostly from years of sharpening on a whet rock and sometimes on the giant concrete block out back where he cleaned the fish and other critters. The handle was dark brown in color, and I imagine it was made of bone.

Daddy Freeman did most everything with his knife. He would skin squirrels and rabbits. Clean fish and cut rope. It served as a screwdriver and fingernail trimmer. He occasionally would take his teeth out and whittle on them. His teeth just never seemed to fit right. He would cut slices off of apples and peaches that came off the trees just out in front of the house. Sometimes he washed his pocketknife and would let it air dry on the windowsill. He mostly just rinsed it off, though.

When I got old enough, I got a pocketknife for Christmas. It wasn't the same as Daddy Freeman's, though. It was too big, and I could hardly unfold the blades. The handle was made of plastic, and I'm not sure if it would cut butter, much less skin a tough squirrel. A dull knife really doesn't have much use. As a young adult I bought my own pocketknife. I picked one out that most closely resembled Daddy Freeman's. It was a good knife, but I lost it somewhere along the way. It never really reached its potential.

Somewhere along the way Daddy Freeman's pocketknife came to be more than a knife. It seemed to reflect Daddy Freeman's life and what I hope for my own future. It was well worn from years of service. It was useful for a variety of things and could handle most everything that was asked of it. With each sharpening it gave up part of itself. It was dependable. It had a look that made it like no other knife, almost having its own personality. It was around for a long time. It was always sharp.

Can't ask for much more than that.

> *Do your best to present yourself to God as one approved by him, a worker who has no need to be ashamed, rightly explaining the word of truth.*
> — 2 Timothy 2:15

# The Gift

We are all amazed from time to time by what children do and think and say. This week I want to share a story about one of our church's little boys. We'll call him Garrett.

One day, Garrett was apparently thinking about Elizabeth, our foster daughter who is about four months old. Now, my family thinks that Elizabeth is pretty special, but we never anticipated how the church would embrace her, especially Garrett. Anyway, Garrett, all on his own, decided that Elizabeth needed something that he had. He got up, without telling anyone, and went to his toy chest and began digging. He grabbed a piggy bank: "Nope, that's not it." Then a yo-yo: "Nope, that's not it." I can imagine toy soldiers and balls and trucks beginning to pile up next to the toy chest as he made his way among the treasures. Finally, seeing the prize, he reached deep down, grabbed it, and ran to his mother with his prized possession. He said he wanted to give it to Elizabeth. Surprised and also smart, his mom washed the gift and brought it to church on Wednesday night. Garrett willingly and joyfully presented to Elizabeth something that had been a favorite of his when he was a baby — a little lamb. It was, indeed, a gift from the heart. First loved by Garrett, now loved by Elizabeth.

You see it, I'm sure. It's a God thing. This little boy did what God did. God's gift of Jesus was a gift from the heart. God reached down deep and found what humanity needed, a Lamb, willingly and joyfully given for you, for me. Loved by the Father and now loved by all who call his name.

*The next day he saw Jesus coming toward him and declared, "Here is the Lamb of God who takes away the sin of the world!"* — John 1:29

# The Fight

I never was much on fighting growing up. There was the kid a couple doors down that I would fuss with from time to time but nothing all that serious. Then I turned fifteen, and one of my not-so-proud moments came around. That's when I had art class with Allen. Allen was short. I was tall. Allen was muscular. I was, well, not. Allen was a bit obnoxious in general, so it came as no big surprise when one day he came over to my project in art class and smeared paint all over it. It did surprise me when I quietly got up from my desk, walked over to his, and crumpled his paper into a ball. What was I thinking?! Allen grabbed me by the shirt and forced me across the room and pinned me down on top of a desk, all in one motion. Lucky for me Mrs. Alred was in the room, and her "Now, boys" was enough to get Allen to release his death grip after a few choice words that only I could hear.

When the bell rang at 3:15 that afternoon, I took my regular path behind the school, headed for the parking lot. Slinking behind me was Allen. My friend Bart looked back and at some point said, "Look out, Howard!" I turned to face my foe, who had already raised his fists up into the fighting position. I had seen such gestures on TV and in the movies and assumed I should do the same, so I did. There we stood with fists clinched, looking every bit like a couple of banty roosters squaring off for a showdown. After some bit of time, Allen took a step closer and drew his fist. Now I was new to this, but it only took a second for me to surmise that this did not bode well for my nose. So I punched him, right in the face. He was stunned for a moment but recovered and came toward me again. POP! My right fist landed squarely on his nose. I was thinking, "Hmmm. This isn't so bad."

It would seem that Allen had made a miscalculation. He thought muscular trumped skinny, and he was right. However, tall trumps short, every time. His twenty-eight-inch arm was no match for my thirty-six-inch reach. So after the third "POP!" Allen bent over and charged me, grabbing me around the waist and pile driving me against the school building. Again, the tall/short thing came into play as I simply wrapped my arm around his head and neck, you know, at waist level. Whenever he moved, I "gently" reminded him there was a brick wall next to us. Bop! Ouch! Bop! Ouch! A teacher finally came around the corner and broke it up, to my great relief. I was beginning to feel like the dog that chased the car and caught it: "What do I do now?"

The next day I was sitting in my friend Charlie's 1957 mint-condition Chevy. Allen came up and got in the seat directly behind me. The bell rang, and the parking lot began to empty as students headed up to class. Again, a friend by the name of Jimmy yelled, "Look out, Howard!" I turned to see Allen with his fist already drawn to hit me. Well, when Jimmy yelled, Allen turned his head to see who it was. POP! I hit him. It hurt me like the dickens because my hands were swollen from the first encounter. Then I said, "Allen, this is stupid." He dropped his hands and agreed. I'd like to say we became friends after that, but we didn't. After all, he was still obnoxious. He did, however, leave me — and my art — alone for the rest of the year.

Not to compare Allen with Satan — oh, what the heck, let's do. Scripture tells us that Satan prowls around like a roaring lion seeking to devour us, me, you, everyone. Like Allen. Like all bullies. The difference is that Allen finally gave up. He recognized that the tall, skinny kid wasn't going to take his obnoxious, bullying behavior and that it was useless to continue banging his head on a brick wall, so to speak. Satan doesn't give up. Like the shark, which must continue moving in order to allow water to pass through his gills, the lion, Satan, keeps moving: tempting, testing, challenging, questioning, enticing, misdirecting, misquoting, and a whole heaping bunch more. We might win a few here and there. Chances are, though, that we'll grow weary, get lazy, or just plain like it and yield. Satan, the evil one, the tempter, that thing will get us with a sucker punch or pin us down on the desk. Not to fret, though. While Mrs. Alred won't be there with her "Now, boys," we know who will be there beside us, forgiving us, strengthening us. It will be Christ, who has won it for us already with a reach that extends from one side of the cross all the way to the other. Thanks be to God.

That was my one and only fight, with fists anyway. There have been many others, with words, though. By the way, sticks and stones (and fists) hurt far less than words. But that's another story.

# The Devil Made Me Do It

I was eight years old at the time and had made my annual summer pilgrimage to Mama Bea's. The farm, of course, belonged to Mama Bea and Daddy Freeman, but everyone called it Mama Bea's, because, well, it was. She was the matriarch of the clan in every sense of the word, and when Mama Bea spoke, we all listened. I was the proud owner of a Daisy BB gun that Santa had gotten from the Sears Roebuck catalogue. Mama Bea had rules that governed the use of BB guns. Don't shoot at the house, don't shoot the dogs and chickens, and don't even think about shooting the purple martins. Cows, snakes, turtles, and other birds were all acceptable targets, especially the snakes and turtles. The purple martins, though, were off limits. Daddy Freeman had built a multi-tiered birdhouse years earlier, and the purple martins had made a permanent summer home of it. Martins were known to return each year to the same birdhouse, and their return became a much-anticipated event. I think the birds' return had become part of the farm's rhythm, just like the planting and the hatching of chicks, so when the martins showed up, we all breathed a collective sigh of relief, knowing that all was well with the world.

One day, my older brother and I were outside with my BB gun. James Freeman was my hero. He was ten years my senior and had been named after Daddy Freeman. He was already out of high school, and I trusted and believed he could do anything. I loved him dearly. He and I were watching the purple martins flying above us at what seemed to be a hundred miles an hour. They were zigging and zagging as they searched and caught insects in mid-air. Then my big brother, my hero, said it: "I bet you can't shoot one." The words "Don't shoot the purple martins" were quickly pushed out of my head, through my ears, and they fell to ground with a thud while the words "shoot one" seemingly grew and grew until they occupied every square inch of my being. Overwhelmed with a sudden sense of urgency, I raised that Daisy BB gun to my shoulder, took aim, and pulled the trigger. Then horror struck. I actually hit one. One of Mama Bea's purple martins fell to the ground. We both ran over to it, and James Freeman bent over and picked up the limp bird. It was motionless, and so was I. My big brother, my hero, held the bird up close to my face, and with a grin that stretched from ear to ear, he said, "Mama Bea is going to get you." He was right. She would get me. What would I ever say to her? I don't really remember what I thought at that moment, but I imagine, being the precocious eight-year-old that

I was, I probably thought that quoting one of the great theologians would do the trick for Mama Bea. Something from Flip Wilson's character, the infamous Geraldine, who said many times "The devil made me do it," seemed most appropriate because whatever excuse I was conjuring up, one thing was certain to me: The person who stood there with that giant grin wasn't just my big brother but seemingly the devil himself.

So there we stood, my brother and I, staring at this motionless bird cupped in his large hands. We both stood there for what seemed an eternity as I was envisioning my Daisy BB gun being placed on the top shelf of the freezer room, there to remain until the pigs out by the barn sprouted wings and flew. Then a miracle occurred. I thought I saw it, but maybe not. No, it did it again. The bird's eye blinked, and then as quickly as it had plummeted to the earth, it took flight, leaving my brother and me standing there with our mouths agape. I watched as the bird mingled with the others in what must have been a homecoming of sorts or an "aviarian" Lazarus experience.

Then I looked down at my brother's hands. They were still cupped as if holding the bird. They were empty, and it was as if it had never happened.

There it is! It is God's lavish grace. Whatever our sin, whatever our misdeed, God's grace comes to us, forgiveness beyond measure, and it is as if it had never happened. As far as the east is from the west; though our sins are like scarlet, we will become pure as snow; if we go to the deepest crevice or the highest pinnacle, we cannot escape the loving, gracious presence of our Lord. The scripture says, In Christ we are adopted according to his will; in Christ we have redemption; in Christ there is forgiveness; in Christ the lavish grace of God is poured out, and it is as if it had never happened. We are God's good creation. We have been clothed with righteousness. You are free to choose…you are free to choose life, life in Christ. My brothers and sisters…you…are…forgiven.

# The Camera

My home in Grenada, Mississippi, was a two-story, red-brick house. The house had three bedrooms, a kitchen, a living room, a dining room, and a single bathroom. All of them were downstairs. Upstairs, the house had never been completed. Consequently, it became a huge attic where all sorts of things found their resting place. As a kid I loved going up into the attic. It was easy as there was an enclosed stairway that went straight up to it. Up in the attic there were canning jars, my dad's wool army uniform, a couple boxes of broken toys, and piles of magazines. A drum set I had received one year found its way into the attic, I suspect rather quickly. Over to one side there were wreaths of plastic flowers that hung loosely on their Styrofoam forms, memories of an infant little sister who died just days after birth. An old black and white television took up one corner. Dad hated throwing things away.

One of my favorite trophies in the attic was an old Kodak box camera. No one thought much about the camera. It had been in the attic forever and was in the box with the broken toys. The camera intrigued me. It was nothing like my Polaroid Swinger, so it was hard for me to imagine how it worked. Oftentimes I would gaze through the scratched square lens and imagine. Surely it had been on safari, had captured wild animals and amazing moments in history. I would snap the shutter and wait on it to spit out a picture like my Swinger did. Nothing ever happened.

High school and college came and went. Seminary took me off to the far country, Texas, and thoughts about the attic and its treasures faded. Mom died. Jana and I met and were married. Life continued. While home for a visit with my dad, the old attic called my name, so up the stairs I went. Nothing much had changed. The old newspaper with JFK's assassination sat right where it had been since 1963. There were a few more magazines. Some tattered quilts had also ascended the stairs. Over in the old cardboard box of broken toys was the camera. I picked it up and stared through the scratched lens. The thought occurred to me: "What if there were pictures inside?" Impossible. Thirty years of Mississippi summer heat and the cold of winter would have ruined them. I found the latch and gently opened the old camera. You guessed it. Inside was a roll of film. As if I had found the ark of the covenant, I carried the film back to a lab in Fort Worth. Three days later there were treasures of immense value. Photographs. Six of them actually. There was a slender young woman on the steps of our house laughing at a really short little boy playing in the snow. Mom and me! Snapshots of a blink in time that was long since gone. Lost moments now remembered. Captured, kept, and now treasured.

God remembers too. It is mentioned over seventy times that God remembers his people. No cameras required! Our Jewish friends have something called the Yizkor prayer. It is a prayer offered for those who have departed. Rabbi Tielson says this of Yizkor: "*Yizkor* is a Hebrew word that means 'He will remember.'" Our memory is most fleeting; it is a blink of the eye. Our memory is short and fuzzy and so very partial. "He will remember" means "God will remember." God is beyond the realm of time, not bound by the clock or the calendar. God is beyond the realm of forgetfulness, for God remembers.

God remembers us. God loves us. God keeps us. God treasures us. Like a mother treasures her child on a snowy day in Mississippi.

# The Big Dance

In my hometown of Grenada, Mississippi, we didn't really have proms. There was an organization known as the "cotillion," which was made up of the young girls in our small community who had reached a certain age, perhaps fifteen or sixteen. There would be a cotillion dance about twice a year, and it fell to the girls to ask the boys to the dance. I suspect the whole event was really a way to perpetuate the segregation of our community, but it might have also been a way to keep certain "elements" from attending. Whatever the reason, it was always a stressful time for me. I wasn't much of a catch, standing at 6' 4" and weighing 140 pounds, unless you needed a light bulb changed. Consequently, the invitations to the big dance weren't exactly filling my mailbox.

One year, though, everything changed. A pretty girl who lived a couple blocks from me asked me to the dance. Nancy (we'll call her) was a year younger than me, and she had always had my eye, but I knew that we were operating out of two different leagues. I never gave the chance of us going out much thought. Nancy had been dating a friend of mine, Al, for a couple years but had recently broken up. Now, nobody wants to be the rebound guy, but when the girl is that dang pretty, most principles go flying out the window. I waved goodbye to mine and gleefully accepted the invitation. Besides, her mother thought I was the best kid in Grenada, and I had high hopes she might have some influence that would increase my future chances.

Have you ever tried to buy a suit for a kid who looks like a drinking straw? My mom had, many times, and she knew there would be nothing in small-town Mississippi, so we headed to Memphis. Twelve hours and six big and tall stores later, we headed south to Grenada with suit in hand. It had been a painful endeavor for both of us, but the chance to dance with Nancy was well worth enduring Mom's grimaces. Did I say dance? That might be an exaggeration that is best not described in any great detail. Feet moved, and hands waved. Enough said.

The big night arrived. I pulled into Nancy's driveway in my 1962 Ford Galaxy with vinyl seats, rubber mats, and AM radio. Nancy's mom greeted me at the door with a big hug and a smile, and then from around the corner came a sight to behold. Nancy appeared, and she had to be the prettiest I had ever seen her. "Wow!" I thought. I handed her the orchid corsage that perfectly matched her gown. Nancy's mom pinned it on, Kodak flashcubes popped, and then we were off to the cotillion.

The evening started well. A few fast dances, one slow dance, a glass of punch, and we sat for a bit. Then "he" came over, Al, that is. "Mind if Nancy and I dance?" he said. I didn't mind. After all, she was my date. She had come with me. What's the harm? Well, I found out. Two hours and too many glasses of punch later, Nancy came over to me. Al was standing a safe distance away.

"Do you mind if Al takes me home?" she asked.

"No, that's fine," I said as I pushed that giant lump in my throat back down to wherever it had come from. I left. Crushed. Betrayed. If you are waiting for a happy ending, there isn't one. But there was a lesson learned. My youth minister had an expression: "People will let you down, always." Then he would say, "But God never will." He was right. Though we may be crushed or feel betrayed, God always desires our good. He will never leave us or forsake us. He is ahead of us, above us, below us, behind us. God is working, always working God's grace in our lives. Thanks be to God, who dances the day we are born and celebrates our lives with us, even through the hard times.

*For he has said, "I will never leave you or forsake you." So we can say with confidence, "The Lord is my helper; I will not be afraid. What can anyone do to me?"* — Hebrews 13:5-6

## The Bad and the Good

Recently I had a conversation with my daughter concerning one of her friends. I had commented that the teen's family had some issues that I was struggling to understand. The parents of the teen seemed uncaring about where the teen was or when or how the teen might get home, if the teen ever got home. Abigail is the least judgmental person I know and in her very direct way said to me, "You didn't have parents with issues." To which I responded almost reflexively, "I did."

My mind then found its way back forty years to 922 Franklin Street. My life was a bit "issue filled." Before I was fourteen, I had been arrested twice. Should have been arrested several more times, but I was sneaky. I wasn't Al Capone, and it was mostly kid stuff, but still. My closest friends at the age of fourteen would all eventually take up residency in the state penitentiary — every one of them, except for one. He committed suicide. On the weekends I could be found on the streets of my small town at almost any hour of the night.

My parents never knew. My sister who will be reading this may even be shocked, just a bit. They didn't know because at home and school, I was the perfect kid. I got almost straight As, mowed the grass, hung up my clothes, was quiet, played baseball, and loved apple pie. But the weekends and summers, well, fourteen-year-olds shouldn't know what I knew or do some of the things I did.

That's the bad.

Let me be clear. In my case the issues that plagued my parents did not revolve around parenting. The lack of supervision was a symptom of other things, and the fact that they really did think I was perfect. I know, hard to believe. My parents loved me, and it was what sustained me during a very scary part of my life.

Then came the brown-haired girl down the street asking me to go to church. I said sure. What sixteen-year-old ever told a cute brown-haired girl no? So I went and never stopped. The church became a safe place. It was a place where youth Sunday school teachers would drone on about Moses or Noah or some other dead guy. But that was ok because those boring youth teachers were there not because they liked teaching (obviously) but because they cared about the youth of the church. Mr. Branscome could kill the best story of the Bible, but he cared.

Then there were the youth. Mostly new faces for me, but they adopted me, the only kid in the group whose parents didn't attend. They let me go out to eat with them. They didn't make fun of my clothes. They invited me over for cards, and we shot baskets together. One night six of them lined the walls of my living room just to say hello and welcome me to church. I became one of them, and it was as if I had always been.

My life changed because of that church, that Sunday school, that youth group in Grenada, Mississippi. I went back not so long ago. I thanked them for all they had done and said, "God saved my soul, but you saved my life." That's what churches do. Thanks be to God for boring teachers and non-judgmental youth. Even for kids with…issues.

And that is the good.

# Sunday School Sweats

In Shake Rag there were two churches when I was growing up: a Baptist and a Methodist church. Mama Bea and Daddy Freeman weren't big churchgoers, but they knew it was important, so occasionally they would send me down the road to attend church. Most of my family was Baptist, I think, but I'm not sure that denominational divisions were all that important in Shake Rag. You just went to church, period. What determined which church you attended on any particular Sunday was a mystery to me then and still is today. Boone's Chapel Methodist Church was the closest one to us. It was also, you may recall, where everyone eventually took up residence for their eternal reward.

One particular Sunday when I was about ten years old, I had made my way to the Methodist church in time for Sunday school. I suppose some cousin or aunt had picked me up and taken me. Boone's Chapel wasn't that big. In fact, as I recall, it had a small, red-brick sanctuary with a couple side rooms, and that was about it. Our little class of ten-year-olds had gathered off to the side of the sanctuary for the morning lesson. Our teacher was a nice lady who was rather young. I'm certain we were related, and I want to say her name was Laura, but I can't be certain. At any rate there were five of us gathered in a semicircle, sitting in folding steel chairs. I remember because I was wearing shorts and my legs kept sticking to the chair. Between the teacher and me there were three girls. All three were sitting very properly in their frilly, white dresses. To my right was another student that I don't remember much about at all, so I'm guessing it must have been a boy.

Somewhere along the way I had learned a critical fact about attending Sunday school: when the teacher asked a question, never look her in the eye. Look down, look out the window, feign reading your Bible, cough a lot, anything, but don't look at the teacher as this assured your name being called upon to answer the question. This strategy had served me well the few times I had attended, but today the teacher had issued a full-blown assault on the class. She was going in order around the semicircle with a question that scared me: "When were you saved, and how did it happen?" Quickly I counted, 1, 2, 3…4. I was fourth. There was time to figure out what the dickens she was talking about when she said "saved." I began to sweat. Her earlier comments seemed to indicate that it had something to do with being a Christian, but it seemed silly to ask such a thing. Didn't she know Mama Bea and Daddy Freeman? They weren't Russians or aliens or anything like that. They were my family, Baptists, Christians, and I had come from that family. Didn't she remember where she lived? America for Pete's sake. Everybody is a Christian. How can I point to a time when I was "saved"? I've always been that way.

The teacher turned to Polly, who sat next to her, and said, "Polly, tell us about when you were saved." Polly said rather snootily, "I was saved on October 23, 1965, when Brother Jim came and preached a revival for our church. I went down the aisle on the second stanza of "Just As I Am" and received Jesus Christ as my personal savior."

"Hmmmmph, teacher's pet," I thought. That had gone way too fast, but it had given me some insight into this "saved" business. There had been a particular date. A decision had been made. Jesus was personal. That was all new to me. Maybe victim number two will shed more light.

"Brenda, tell us about when you were saved," said the teacher.

"That's not a fair question," she responded. With those five words I felt like a bale of Daddy Freeman's hay had been lifted from my shoulders. She was stalling. She didn't have an answer either. I was set free. The teacher continued to prod her but to no avail. The buzzer rang, indicating class was over, and I pulled my sweaty legs free from the steel chair and bolted. It would be a long time before I would go back to Sunday school.

Although that experience was most uncomfortable for me, I count it as one of the pivotal times in my spiritual formation. It would be another seven years before I would become a Christian. The Spirit would use that Sunday school teacher, my grandfather, a few friends, and a couple more occasions to nudge me along. I suspect most believers can reflect back and see such "Spirit proddings" in their faith development. Perhaps we would all do well to sit down with a pen and paper and remember those people and events that God has used in our lives.

*What then is Apollos? What is Paul? Servants through whom you came to believe, as the Lord assigned to each. I planted, Apollos watered, but God gave the growth.... For we are God's servants, working together; you are God's field, God's building.* — 2 Corinthians 3:5-6, 9

# Snakes and Gardens

My grandparents and almost all of my mother's extended family lived in Shake Rag, a community out in Chickasaw County, about ten miles from Okolona, Mississippi. Okolona is about ten miles from Verona, which is just a stone's throw from Tupelo. Most of you, if you are southern and at least forty-five years old, will know that Tupelo is the birthplace of Elvis.

My grandmother, Mama Bea, had a garden. It was always Mama Bea's garden even though my grandfather, Daddy Freeman, did as much work in it as she did. I remember Mama Bea making Daddy Freeman get up out of his chair one day to go till the garden. He didn't like it one bit, and when the tiller wouldn't start, he took a hammer and started pounding on it. Better the tiller than Mama Bea, I thought, because I was quite certain Mama Bea could take him.

Anyway, they had a garden that to any eight-year-old looked as if the entire world's population could be fed from it. Its rows yielded corn, tomatoes, eggplants, okra, squash, watermelons, onions, potatoes, and most everything else that could be planted, grown and eaten, canned, or frozen. The garden also had a huge section that was the strawberry patch. I can still see Mama Bea stooped over in the strawberry patch, sweat dripping from her face as she would pull weeds and later as she searched for the big, red berries. Daddy Freeman would be off in another part tilling, or hammering, whatever was appropriate for that particular day and the demeanor of the tiller.

I wasn't there the day that it happened. My memories of the encounter rely on the memories and stories of my mother and others. Mama Bea was meticulously going through the strawberry patch when she felt a sting on her hand. Now, I don't know if it happened this way or not, but what I picture is Mama Bea straightening up and holding her hand out at arm's length and there being a water moccasin with fangs still imbedded in her hand. How it happened, I don't know, but one thing was for certain: two were in the garden, and only one was going to leave alive. Mama Bea hated snakes and was a fierce opponent when her hoe was nearby. I'm certain that snake figured out pretty quickly that it had bitten off more than it could chew.

The next several days Mama Bea's life hung in the balance. She had been transported to Houston, Mississippi, for medical treatment. There was no antivenom, but this southern woman was strong as an ox. She overcame the poison that had violated her body just as she had dispatched that snake. I don't remember if there was a strawberry patch the following year.

Snakes and gardens just don't seem to go together, do they? Eve discovered that, as did Adam. We want to enjoy God's good creation, and somehow it gets mucked up on occasion by snake-like critters. Some might call it temptation, maybe even sin. It just gets in the way and can sting, even resulting in the loss of life, spiritual or physical. If we only had a champion, someone who could wield a spiritual hoe as Mama Bea had and dispatch sin and temptation before its sting. If only there was someone who could go ahead of us, searching and destroying, as it were. If only there was someone...

*The sting of death is sin, and the power of sin is the law. But thanks be to God, who gives us the victory through our Lord Jesus Christ.*
— 1 Corinthians 15:56-57

## Scars

When our family lived in Waco, Texas, Abigail had a close friend named Jessica. Jessica's family had come to live in the United States illegally but had made inroads in becoming legal immigrants. They were poor and stuffed their five-member family into a tiny house not far from where we lived. One December night the dad awoke to find the Christmas tree on fire. He and his wife scrambled to get everyone through a window to safety. They all made it, but Jessica was severely burned on her hands and face. The scars that were left on her face were severe, and her hands were misshapen from the flames.

In the following years Abigail and Jessica became best friends. Sleepovers, birthday parties, and play days always included Jessica. Jessica was able to teach Abigail how to ride a bicycle after I had in frustration vowed never to try again! Because of their closeness, we were able to follow Jessica's medical progress as doctors worked to remove the scarring from her face and hands. For her face they used a procedure where balloons were inflated in her cheeks for several months at a time so that new skin would grow. The new skin would then be stretched over her cheeks to replace the scarred areas. That, along with the surgeries to her hands, was very painful, especially for a seven-year-old.

Not once did I ever hear Jessica or her parents complain. Jessica's scarring and occasional chipmunk-like appearance, which was no doubt a source of cruelty by other children, never seemed to bother her. The pain of the surgeries never reduced her smile to a frown. The entire family was a source of great inspiration.

Wouldn't it be grand if we could all deal with our scars the way Jessica was able to? We all have them, scars, that is. They are scars that aren't seen on the body but are found on the soul. They are the remnants and reminders of difficult childhoods, broken relationships, poor self-esteem, and a host of other reasons. Often, the scars are worn with pride. We cling to them because they bring us attention or sympathy. Other times we carry the scars because the pain of healing is greater than our willingness to do the hard work of removing them. I'm sure there are many more reasons too. We enjoy them and at the same time wish they weren't there.

God desires, I believe, that we should let them go. Release them so we can live more freely and not be bound by the past. Heal them so they don't continually remind us of our defeats and losses. God can heal us. Sometimes, like Jessica, it may require others as God's healing agents: spiritual friends, counselors, and even doctors. But with God and the same hard work that Jessica put into her healing, we too can be healed. After all, God knows a thing or two about scars.

*...by his bruises we are healed.* — Isaiah 53:5

# Possum

When we lived in Waco, Texas, we had a friend and church member who was quite the character. He had been educated at Baylor University and had taught biology for a while and then worked a few years as a restaurant inspector. When we knew him, he was in his late fifties and had been dubbed "Possum" by another friend. I'm not sure why he was called Possum; he just was. Somewhere along the way Possum had decided that the traditional lifestyle was not for him. He didn't have any family and never married, although he did have a girlfriend for a brief time while we were living in Waco. He gave up his job and mowed yards for a living. You could see him most any summer day in his little pickup hauling his push mower, rake, and broom up and down the streets of Waco. He still lived in the house he had grown up in and inherited from his parents. Possum had an odd way about him that endeared him to everyone and reflected a deep wisdom that only comes from a life well lived. He was fond of saying, "Don't criticize your enemies until you've walked a mile in their shoes. Then you'll be a mile away from them, and you'll have their shoes."

Possum frequently pulled into my driveway to chat. He would go to the door and then go back and stand by his pickup, waiting on me to come out. I could never get him to come in the house. We talked about many things: sermons, the weather, mutual friends, politics, the "Missus," and a hundred other topics. One of those other topics was the vacation Possum was planning. Possum was always planning a vacation, usually to Wyoming to go fly-fishing. We would discuss the route, the things he would need, even settle on a date. The day would inevitably come, Possum would pack, loading his pickup with every conceivable item, and then go to bed to rest before the early start the next day. Possum would get up bright and early, go out, and unload his pickup, almost every time. Some of the guys at church even promised to pay for the trip if he would just go. One year, he actually left town headed north. He got as far as Fort Worth, about 100 miles, and turned around and came home. As far as I know, Possum has never made it to Wyoming.

The trip was obviously very important to Possum or he would not have planned it so meticulously every year. However, his reasons for not going were even more important, at least to him. We don't like it, but the fact is that many of us are just like Possum. We make big plans, especially this time of year, to make changes in our lives. We make meticulous plans to jolt us out of our ruts only to fall back on excuses for the status quo. Too much work. Not enough time. Next year for sure. Something came up. It's my children. It's my parents. The list really can be long, can't it?

Maybe it's time to stop making resolutions and work on making covenants. A covenant is a promise, not a wish. It's a promise to another, or to God, and sometimes both. Maybe it's time we see our need for change not as a physical or mental issue but as a spiritual issue. Give it to God. Regularly pray about it. Be accountable to another. If you fail at first, don't consider yourself a failure. God doesn't! Continue working and praying and working. Allow the Spirit access to empower.

Let me know how it goes.

See you in Wyoming.

# Party Line

Mama Bea didn't seem to get mad about much. She would get mad at the chickens for coming up on the porch and leaving, well, you know. Mama Bea's porch was generally as clean as her kitchen floor, except when the chickens visited. She would fly out the back door with her broom swinging and in her loudest voice call, "Shuhhhhhhh. Git outta he-uh!" You already know she got mad at Daddy Freeman from time to time, and of course snakes always incurred her wrath.

She also got a little more than peeved at the lady down the road. Back when communications technology was just a step above two tin cans and a string, there were party lines. If you lived in town or out in the country, you often had to share a telephone line with a neighbor, sometimes several. Each house had a phone with a distinctive ring that let you know the call was for you — perhaps a long ring followed by a short ring or two short rings or just one ring. You get the picture. You would often have to wait to place a call while the other party on the line finished their conversation. And it was understandable that occasionally you might pick up on someone else's ring. If you did, you just hung up and left them to their private conversation, unless you were the lady down the road. The lady down the road was fond of listening in. Mama Bea would be on the line with someone when she would hear the familiar "click" that indicated someone had picked up. She would wait for the second click to indicate that the neighbor was off the line and not listening in. Sometimes the wait was longer than others. Sometimes Mama Bea would say, "I'll call you back later." Then she would hang up, and there would be mumbling about nosey busybodies listening in. I suspect she wanted to say, "Git outta he-uh!" before hanging up.

It seems that we've come full circle in our technology. We have the ability to actually invite others to join in on our phone conversations. At home or on my cell, I can just push a button or two and invite others into the conversation. On my cell I can even tell people my geographic location, and I can let them see me and my surroundings. I recently pushed the wrong button and allowed someone to see Jana sleeping in bed, all covered up fortunately. Don't tell Jana.

What if everyone was always able to hear our conversations, invited or not? How would that change what we say? Perhaps we might be kinder and less gossipy. Maybe our Sunday dinner conversation would be more affirming and less critical. Even our good-natured jabs during football season might change to more encouraging comments than "We gotcha!" tones. Of course we know God hears all of it: the kind and the critical. We, or perhaps I should really say "I," like to think God only hears me when I dial him up. He only sees me when I push my "FaceTime" button on the cell. Then it's just him and me. We tend to forget that our thoughts and words are on a party line when it comes to God. No invitations necessary. No click to remind us God is around. God just is.

This week, I'm going to work on that. I'll try to talk more to God and less "about" others. I'll try to be encouraging, affirming, and positive. Let's all give it a try. Others will notice, maybe even be reminded themselves of a need to tweak their words a bit. God will be pleased.

Hmmmm. I wonder if God's ring is two shorts or one long.

*Let no evil talk come out of your mouths, but only what is useful for building up, as there is need, so that your words may give grace to those who hear.*
— Ephesians 4:29

## Ol' Mike

One of my favorite sports on the farm in Shake Rag would make most folks cringe. It was snake hunting, and there were plenty of snakes around, especially water moccasins. With seven ponds and a creek you could find a snake most any day. You may remember that it was Mama Bea who was bitten by a snake once while picking strawberries. Whether it was the snake assault upon my family or just plain fun, I loved to go snake hunting.

Daddy Freeman had an English Setter named Mike. Mike was an old dog as long as I can remember. Mike was a good friend, and he loved to hunt snakes as much as I did. As soon as I came out of the house with Daddy Freeman's single shot .22 caliber rifle, he knew it was time to go hunting. We would head off across the pasture to one of the larger ponds. If I was lucky and the snake wasn't, I would spot one swimming across the water. I would then send out a barrage of bullets that either mortally wounded it or scared it to death. Most often, though, Mike and I would walk around the edges of the pond in search of our prey. It would be quite obvious when Mike spied the evil little demon. His tail would start wagging, and he would approach the edge of the water with a kind of hesitant jumping motion. With my command of "Get him, Mike," he eventually would make a quick grab, and out of the water would come the snake. Mike and the dragon would then do battle. Mike always won. Almost.

There was one time when Mike didn't win, but he didn't lose either. As a matter of fact, Mike refused to even challenge the snake. We were making our usual rounds when his tail started wagging and he began moving in such a way that I knew there was a snake on the edge of the pond. I couldn't see it to save my life, literally. He jumped this way, then that way, never venturing within a foot of the water's edge. Mike had never been afraid before. I then spied the serpent's nose just protruding at the very edge of water. BLAM! BLAM! BLAM!

After a bit, Mike finally reached into the water and began pulling on the moccasin. He pulled and pulled. Finally, I helped him with a stick, but once it was on the bank, it scared the jeebers out of me. It was no longer part of this world (if it ever was); it was just that it was the biggest snake I had ever seen. As long as my rifle and as big around as my leg, I was certain that it could have swallowed Mike in a single gulp, not to mention the saber-length teeth that would have yielded a deadly blow. We both escaped that day.

Ever since that thing happened in the garden of Eden, snakes and humanity have been at odds. Didn't do much for our relationship with God either. Come to think of it, it messed up humanity all the way around. The Bible calls it sin. We're more apt to call it a mistake or a bad choice or to just say we messed up. We don't like the word "sin" any more than we like snakes. We know that to God, sin is sin. Period. But we like to think in terms of big sins and little sins. I tend to think of little sins as things that hurt for a little while, like losing my temper or, these days, eating too much salt. It hurts me or briefly interrupts a good friendship, but that's about all. Then there are big sins. You and I don't do those. Murder. Adultery. Idol worship. Then there are those sins that start out little and become big. Like David peeking at Bathsheba. It was just a peek. But it turned into murder.

Ol' Mike had a pretty good nose for trouble. He knew that despite his expertise in dispatching serpents, he had met his match. I wish I could be that smart all the time. The truth is, God is right, as usual. Sin is sin. Period. Little, big, or in-between sin is always bigger than we can handle. There is no such thing as a small disruption in relationships. Even if it doesn't show, it tends to linger, forever. We need something that goes BLAM! so we can eradicate the situation before it bites us. There is something. Something far better than Daddy Freeman's .22 caliber rifle. Even if we commit our "bad choice," God says, "Here. It's yours." It's GRACE! GRACE! GRACE!

And it is more than enough.

*The serpent tricked me...* — Genesis 3:13

*For by grace...it is the gift of God.* — Ephesians 2:8

# Luggage

When I was a little guy, I had a red bicycle with a wire basket on the front. It wasn't very cool. Spider bikes were making their way into stores, and they were way cooler. You remember those. They had the long handlebars and the banana seat.

One year Mother's Day was approaching, and I decided to get something special for my mom. Up until then, my gifts had been handmade cards that the teachers at school had forced the classes to design and make. I was all grown up now and needed to do something more. So I went to my room and got my safe. My safe was a wooden box that Dad had brought home from the railroad, and I had put a lock on it that I had luckily gotten when I put a penny in the trinket machine outside the Big Star grocery. Inside the box were my treasures: a piece of crystal-looking rock, notes for girls that I had never delivered, a few school pictures of those same girls, a couple special marbles, and my money. Now, make no bones about it, I was a wealthy kid. I had a bag full of coins that I had gotten when my grandmother died, and it totaled almost twenty dollars. I intended to spend it all on Mom.

Out the door I went with a pocket full of money. I flung my ten-year-old lanky legs over my bike and pedaled to the Morgan and Lindsey store. It was certain that an appropriate gift could be found there. No expense would be spared. As soon as I walked in, a set of luggage that was on sale caught my eye. The bag contained just barely enough money. I completed my purchase and carefully balanced the three-piece set of green (cardboard) luggage on the wire basket and handlebars and pedaled home. I made it and hid the luggage under the bed before Mom got home. I could hardly wait. Each day dragged by as my excitement and pride in my gift mounted. Every morning and afternoon I would pull out the luggage just to make sure it was still there.

Mother's Day morning, I jumped out of bed, pulled out the luggage, stacked it, and made my way to the dining room. "Happy Mother's Day!" Mom smiled. I smiled. Mom cried. I gloated. The perfect gift. It was a set of very cheap luggage, but it was filled with all the love that boys have for their moms.

The luggage sat there in the dining room all day on display. At some point my parents asked how I could possibly afford to buy such a wonderful set of luggage. I explained that the money in my safe had been just enough. Silence.

Then another round of thank yous was expressed, and the day ended as the best Mother's Day ever.

Mom used that cheap cardboard luggage for years. It finally fell apart. The heat from the attic was just too much for the glue that held it together. Not a single time did Mom ever tell me that the money I had used was all silver dollars from my grandmother's estate and was probably worth two or three hundred dollars, a lot of money for a working-class family. The gift joyfully given had been far more costly than I had imagined.

The season of Advent is close at hand, and we will reflect and remember a little baby being born in a manger. We will remember and celebrate the gift that was joyfully given and filled with all the love of the Father. Remember, too, that while the gift was freely given to us, it was also costly, more costly than Mary, Joseph, and all those who gathered in the stable could ever imagine. So this year, remember. Remember and give thanks for family, for gifts given and received, and for a Savior.

*For God so loved the world that he gave his only son...* — John 3:16

# Loretta

Today is beautiful. The sky is as blue as any I have seen over Huntsville. A red wasp is warming itself on my window as the sun's rays lap at my feet. The colors of fall are beginning to show themselves, teasing us for the show that will soon take center stage upon our mountains. Life is good.

With so much of life popping all around, I shouldn't be thinking about death. My aunt and uncle celebrated fifty years of marriage on Sunday. Their anniversary was announced in *The Commercial Appeal*, the Memphis newspaper. In the announcement they list their children, Stephen, Fred, and Loretta. Loretta died from a brain tumor forty-one years ago this month. I remember it well, too well. My own personal pain and grief were great for someone only eleven years old. Even now, as I write, I am aware of the grief still. My family grieved heavily. Uncle Fred and Aunt Linda were devastated. Vivid in my mind were the hundreds of law enforcement officers who lined the streets and highway as the procession made its way to the cemetery. They came from all over the state to honor their brother, their fellow officer, and his family.

The red wasp is still on my window.

The apostle Paul asks, "Where, O death, is your sting?" Paul was writing about those who die, but what about those who remain? One day, some day, that sting will be no more. But for now that sting hurts like, well, like hell. Because it is, hell, that is. If hell is, at minimum, separation from God and love, then the death and separation from those we love gives us some insight into what hell might be. It is a painful place that you would think would make us all bitter or angry or mean. Some don't believe in hell. I don't want to, but I see it, too often, in the papers, in the lives of people, in death.

Loretta was special. I suppose all our children are. However, Loretta showed unusual grace for a seven-year-old who was dying. It was of such significance that her surgeon reflected on the lessons he had learned from her during an interview on national television many years later. At the time I was too young and too far away to recognize her gift. However, I have seen such grace in others. I have seen it in my aunt and uncle, who bore the pain graciously over the years. It is evident in the lives of the saints we honored yesterday, good people who are now gone, not before knowing great sorrow, yet still living graciously. Even today, in our congregation, the sting of death still resides, but oh the grace, the grace that is a witness to me and our community that death's pain is real but it is not the victor.

Hell will not have its way. Because of God's grace, the love of Christ, the healing power of the Spirit, and the fellowship of the community of faith, we can join our voices and together say, "Life is good; thanks be to God."

The red wasp is gone.

# Looking Back

Our foster daughter Chyna is almost eight months old. She is a delight. Her face appears to be a perpetual ray of sunshine, and she greets not just every day, but almost every moment with a smile. At 4:30 in the morning there tend to be more frowns and notes of discontent than smiles. She has learned that enough of that will land her in the bed with Jana, all cozy and warm. The coos and smiles quickly return. However, that tends to push me over to the edge of the bed and an uncomfortable wait for the alarm to sound at 6:30.

Last night I decided it was time to, as Barney Fife said, "Nip it, nip it, nip it." So I prepared her bed at the usual time but added a little extra fluffiness to help it more closely resemble our bed. We put her to bed, and with only a few grumbles she was fast asleep. I thought, "Heh heh. I gotcha." Then I smugly looked forward to a full night's rest. At 4:20, there was a whimper. I thought, "She'll think she is already in our bed and fall back to sleep." At 4:25 there was a string of attention-getters. I thought, "This is a test. She'll yield and fall asleep." At 4:30 there was a full-blown cacophony being hurled from her bed toward ours. Not wanting to lose the battle completely, I went and got her, sat in the rocking recliner, and prayed…and prayed…and prayed. Eyes as big as saucers looked up at me as if to say, "Bring it on, Big Boy." So I rocked. About every three minutes she sat up, looked longingly over at the bed, laid her head back in my arms, and with those big saucer eyes all but said, "Why are you doing this to me?" She eventually fell asleep around 5:30 A.M. We'll see what tonight brings.

Many of you know that I have a medical condition that is potentially serious but for now is held in check. Part of the prescription for keeping it in check is a change in diet. Specifically, I have eliminated salt from my diet. I am allowed two grams per day. If you have ever looked at a can of soup, you know that those meager ten ounces contain enough salt by itself to account for about one-third of my daily allotment. A lot of my favorite foods are now taboo: pizza, barbeque, nachos, hotdogs, French fries, pickles, roast beef sandwiches, and Mexican/Chinese/Italian and most everything else in any restaurant, to name a few. Most days it's no big deal. Some days it is a big deal. I get cravings and remember the days of carefree sodium consumption. I sit up and look back at the days when things were different and wonder, "God, why are you doing this to me?" I know in my mind that God didn't do anything to me. It was a genetic something that I inherited. But still, I got to yell at somebody.

A lot happened in 2010. Change, that is. Something significant in our lives was lost that will forever leave us in a different, often uncomfortable place. Loss is hard to accept. The Israelites looked back and wished they had never left Egypt: "At least we could eat something besides manna back there." They had lost a way of life that was familiar and in some ways comfortable. They yelled at Moses and at God. I like to think that God is okay with that. Yelling, that is. After all, sometimes we need to yell at somebody, and who better than the one who loves us unconditionally, who came to live among us, who understands our pain, who sees our faces as a constant ray of sunshine, even in our most agonizing moments.

# Learning to Drive

Abigail is learning to drive. I'm learning patience.

Now that she has her permit, she has staked a claim to the front left seat of the car — the driver's side. You'd think the girl had just crossed hundreds of miles of treacherous terrain whilst fightin' the natives in order to possess this small piece of real estate. She thinks she has some inalienable right to drive on every occasion. Last night it was time to leave church, so she assumed the throne of teen independence and reached for the keys. I yielded, knowing that to protest that it was dark and that I hadn't brought the defibrillator wasn't much of an excuse to not let her drive. So off we went. It is my habit to not speak too loudly about her driving but to offer quiet, assuring words of correction. There was that one time that "STOP!" was necessitated by circumstances that are better not spoken of…ever again. Anyway, I was offering a few suggestions when Zackary spoke up from the back seat and said matter-of-factly, "Abigail, objects in mirror are closer than they appear." Now, Zackary could not see the mirror from his seat, and it was dark. Apparently he had committed the words to memory, waiting on an appropriate time to offer his suggestion from his vast wealth of driving experience. Normally, that would have been enough to send Abigail clamoring over the seat to put Zackary in a hold that would make the World Wrestling Federation proud. However, she was concentrating on driving, so she ignored him.

"Objects in mirror are closer than they appear." What was he thinking? No doubt he wanted to be helpful, but what was Zackary offering? Maybe a warning, as in, "Abigail, that Mack truck is really close." Maybe it was a statement of fact, as in, "Abigail, that's a Mack truck, not a Tonka toy." Who knows?

Jesus may have found the same words useful in his day. Actually, it seems he may have said something sort of similar. "Objects in mirror are closer than they appear" or "The kingdom of God is at hand." If you are like me, I tend to think that the kingdom of God is a good ways out there. It is far enough for me to have time to get things right. We (I) talk like we believe the kingdom will one day come, but come on, really? We've got time. Objects in mirror are cl…o…ser than… Oops! You don't even have to read the fine print. It's as plain as that Mack truck. Jesus said, "The kingdom of God is *at hand.*" That means "at arm's reach" or "it can be touched." In other words, the kingdom is here! God's kingdom, God's reign, is now. We're not waiting for it; we're living it. The question is,

"How are we living it?" "Thy kingdom come, Thy will be done," we pray. How about we all climb down from our own throne of independence and let God... well, you know.

# Leaning

One Easter I walked into my office after worship to find an anonymous card on my desk. Ministers don't usually like anonymous mail. Typically it is sent by some irate individual who is taking issue with a sermon, the sanctuary temperature, a misspoken word, a failure to say hello, or, well, you get the idea. This time, though, the anonymous missal brought a smile to my face. The front of the card portrayed a 1950s-looking preacher proclaiming, "Today's Easter sermon is…" Upon opening the card the sentence is completed: "Where the heck have you been since Christmas?" (It's not a direct quote, mind you. You understand.) While the card did not capture my feelings (wink, wink), it does reflect the "trade talk" of my profession. Ministers wish that every Sunday the pews were packed and the 400-plus who attended Easter morning here would be back next Sunday. We know that won't happen, though, so we (I) are grateful for whoever comes on any given Sunday.

Every Easter I am stirred by what happens in the sanctuary. The children's procession of fresh flowers transforms a wooden cross into a living symbol of the resurrection. The choir with organ, piano, and orchestra gives audible expression to my feelings of gratitude and joy. And then there are the faces. All 400-plus of them gathered together for at least this one Sunday to worship and thank God for the gift of immeasurable love and grace. This year I was struck by not just the joy of the gathered body but also by the sadness. Over in one corner is a recovering addict. Close to the front a grieving spouse. Over there is a divorced person. Another suffers from chronic pain. Back in the back a young couple grieving the loss of an infant. Still another grieving the loss of a teen. On and on the litany went, fresh wounds, old wounds not yet healed, all gathered to celebrate the risen Christ even in the midst of their own struggles to be resurrected from the dark tomb of loss and suffering.

One person in particular caught my eye. Sitting there in the midst of great grief, she was flanked on either side by two very close, good friends. I was reminded of the paralyzed man who was brought to Jesus and lowered through a roof. That man, on that day, rose up and walked away a new person, and it started with a few "friends" being present and taking him to Jesus. That's what I saw Easter, among the faces. I saw people all over the sanctuary in pain, paralyzed if you will, surrounded by good friends. Each of them was sustained by grace-filled presence. And in spite of the darkness that surrounds them, they are in fact being resurrected as the body of Christ.

So let us all in our own suffering learn to lean on the arms that are outstretched from friends who are a grace-filled presence in our lives. Let us also learn to lean on those everlasting arms and see "how bright the path grows from day to day."

Leaning.

# Valentines

At the age of fifty-three I can count on one hand the number of valentines I have had over the years, at least of the romantic variety. My first was Debbie. Debbie was a cute little blonde-haired girl in the third grade. She lived a few blocks from my house, and every afternoon I would get on my spider bike and ride down to her house. There was a pile of loose gravel out front, and I would race to the gravel, slam on the brakes, and skid 180 degrees. Debbie never let on that she liked me, but I'm certain that secretly she was madly in love with me, mostly because of my great bicycle skills. Next came Cathy. No details here except to say that in the sixth grade she held my heart in her hand, looked me in the eye, and crushed it, with a big smile on her face. Pam and I were an item in high school, until the high school jock began paying attention to her and I was history. I still think I could have taken him. Jennifer was my college valentine for about two years. We were sort of serious for a time, but it didn't last. We parted ways when I left for seminary. I was a Baptist preacher; she was a Methodist preacher's daughter. Enough said.

It was in seminary that I met the love of my life, but not my last valentine. Jana and I were introduced by a mutual friend in October, went on our first date December 31, were engaged on March 15, and married on December 15, 1984. My life changed forever. She was and is a gift from God.

Another valentine came along July 18, 1993, when Abigail was born and again when Zackary joined us. There have been others. Guys and gals. I think of Kerwin, Hubert, Kim, Rose, and my friend Buddy who died a few years ago. As a youth Mrs. Corey taught me about Christ and God's love. There are the many senior adults of our church and so many friends. All of them loved by me and have given love in return.

Saint Valentine has several myths surrounding him. No one truly knows much about him or how he became associated with a day filled with hearts and Cupids. One tradition that I like is that during the reign of Claudius II, someone named Valentinus helped Christians in need, especially those being persecuted by the emperor. That, for me, is a better picture and cause for celebrating Valentine's Day. It is not the people who have made my heart go pitty-pat or even thumpity-thump, but those who have helped others. When Jana and I were married, we made lifetime promises that we would love and nurture each other, helping the other become the best that God intended. She has certainly kept her promise.

I have tried to keep mine. There are many others in my life who have also fed my soul: being present in times of great sadness, teaching me about grace, keeping me attentive to God's path, and being Christ's presence.

Celebrate Valentine's Day the next time it rolls around. A pretty card is a good start. But also sit down with pen and paper and remember the many people who have graced your life. Recount specific ways they have been Christ's presence for you. Thank God for each of them, and if you can, thank them. It will be the best Valentine's gift they will receive this year.

# Quirky Kid

Five years ago next month, a little boy came to our house for the first time. A friend of a friend had mentioned that we might be interested in adopting. So they dropped him off for a trial run, sort of. He had all his fingers and toes. He had huge brown eyes. On the back of his hands were scars. I'm not sure he even knew they were there or that they shouldn't be there. They just were. They spoke volumes to us, though. This little boy had already traveled a long road from being abused as an infant and then passed off to a strange family for safekeeping and even now was being passed off again. He must have wondered why and for how long. Would this be another layover on the journey, or would this house, this family, offer sanctuary from a nomadic life that began with wounds from a world of sin?

We soon discovered the little boy was, well, active. Way too active. Off the chart active. He didn't walk through the house; he bounced like the super ball I had as a kid. ADHD were the letters that were attached to his medical file. Drugs were in order. It had to be either Adderall for him or Prozac for us. He needed help more than we did. Being tossed from kindergarten every other day would not be a résumé builder for the first grade. ADHD kids have difficulties in many ways. They are usually developmentally behind as much as three years. They can't focus. They are often labeled as lazy because they can't concentrate to do their work, so they do nothing. And with a brain that never rests, they can have behavior issues. In lay terms, they are trouble-makers. Labels, discipline, being ignored, considered lazy, and not being able to relate to peers are bound to leave scars. These are not as evident as the others but are scars nonetheless.

The boy still displayed unusual behavior, even for an abused child with ADHD. We had every test done that could be done. Nothing. Nada. No one could tell us anything definitive. There were terms thrown around by professionals that described a developing Hannibal Lecter. About then we adopted the boy, knowing that his journey was getting longer and harder every day. We hoped that permanency would help. It didn't. Tortuous meltdowns. Chairs being thrown. Screams that "the music is too loud," "it's too cold," "I have to eat before I can put on my socks," constant whining, ignoring adults, reclusive behavior, repetitive sounds, intense desire to be right, correcting adults, melting down when corrected, and oh so much more.

Then Jana said the right word: "Asperger's." He was tested, and that was it. The brown-eyed boy had Asperger's syndrome. It explained it all. We were concerned and relieved at the same time. Finally, a diagnosis. Wait. What the heck is Asperger's? It's a form of autism, and that's about all I know for now. We are learning, almost daily. What we do know is that you can't see it. It's not a scar on a hand that explains a world gone wrong. It's invisible. What we see are symptoms. Not everyone gets it. Recently a teacher called the boy by a derogatory epithet when what she was observing was a symptom, not a "normal" kid making bad choices. I was angry. I wanted to say, "Look at the scars," but there aren't any that can be seen. Not for this. I realized too that this would be part of his journey. Misunderstandings, assumptions, judgments, and labels that he is "quirky," if people are kind, will be his lot.

Thomas asked Jesus if he could see his scars. Jesus showed him his hands. The scars verified for Thomas that it was indeed Jesus, but for me the scars speak volumes about a world of sin. A world that is not what God intended. It is a world where tornadoes rip through towns, wars begin over greed, adults are left on the streets to live, and quirky children are teased and maligned. It is a world where children on the other end of the autism spectrum are locked away behind blank stares. It is a world where adults sometimes behave like children. It is a world…, well, you get it. What holds it together for me is the unassailable belief that God will and does continue to work. Creation continues. Grace somehow brings humanity forward even at the almost intolerable pace of a snail. So thanks be to God for not giving up on quirky humanity and little boys who say, "No, Dad, it's 8:31, not 8:30."

# Phone Call from God

Jana is my wife. You may know her as friend, minister, sister-in-law, or any number of different titles. You know her in those different roles, but you may not know all there is to know about her. Come to think of it, I don't think I do either. Nonetheless, you may or may not know that Jana has an unusual organizational system. She has piles. There is a pile in her office. There is a pile in one corner of the bedroom (all that I can tolerate). She has a pile in her car. There is a pile in her purse. The garage doesn't have a pile; it is a pile. She knows where most things are although I do hear a lot of "Have you seen..." and "Where is my..." or "Can you bring me some keys?"

Jana also is technologically, ummmm, deficient (?). She bemoans her laptop and occasionally commands that the demons leave for some herd of pigs or chipmunks. It is always broken but somehow miraculously heals itself when it is handed to me with a "Fix it!" demanded. She is convinced that her cell phone was invented to terrorize her, even though she loves spending time with it and reaching out to Texas or across town. It seems to buzz when it should ring. It dings when it should vibrate. She hasn't figured out voicemail just yet, so I suggest you never leave her one.

Yesterday her organizational skills and technowizardry intersected. An open Coke that was in her purse (read, "pile") spilled in the purse/pile and baptized her cell phone. While I'm sure she would have been glad that the cell phone was finally saved and baptized, the cell phone objected and stopped working. Again, technology had failed in its performance and let her down. We let it dry overnight, stickiness and all. Today I called her, and (surprise!) she answered. The cell phone was working. Here's the short conversation: *Hello.* Hi, your phone works. *Yeah, although I wasn't sure at first.* Why? *When I put the battery in and turned it on, a passage from the Bible popped up.* What did it say? *I don't know; it was from Deuteronomy, so I cleared it.* Maybe it was a word from God. *Well, if it was, I hung up on him!*

Oops! There we are, right? Hanging up on God, I mean. Every so often we are fortunate enough to be in tune, on the same wavelength, listening, or just finally paying attention to God. Then comes a word. The problem is, we don't like it. It wasn't what we were praying for. It wasn't what we expected. We don't want to do it. We are inconvenienced. So we hang up on God. We hit redial, hoping to get someone else in customer service, but the word is still the same.

We would ask for a supervisor, but, well, you know. Wouldn't it be a good thing if we would only hear it, receive it, and respond? If only it were that easy.

This is the last week of Advent. Each of the four weeks of Advent has a word associated with it. This week is "love." Let's do our best in the stores, at work, at school, and at home to take that as a word from God. Let's all love, in God's name. Let's all love, in the power of the Spirit. Let's all love, as much as the Child was loved and loves us still. Don't hang up; hang on, and be a loving presence in your world.

*Little children, let us love, not in word or speech, but in truth and action.*
— 1 John 3:18

# It Was a Miracle

Daddy Freeman was always the first one out of bed. He had chores to do. He had animals to feed and cows to milk by hand. Mama Bea's feet were usually second to hit the floor. She had mouths to feed, in particular me and Daddy Freeman. She usually would fry something: homemade sausage, home-cured bacon, or an occasional rabbit or squirrel. Along with that would be eggs that came from the henhouse and cathead biscuits, which would be paired with homemade butter and jelly. I think my cholesterol level just jumped twenty points remembering all of that.

Now, don't let the term "cathead biscuits" bother you. They weren't really catheads, although I do remember having a fried squirrel head a time or two. This morning meal would be washed down with the milk that Daddy Freeman had freed from the cow the previous day. Daddy Freeman would have coffee that he first cooled in the saucer. All of this would be ready by the time Daddy Freeman walked in from milking the cow. He would bring in the milk in a bucket that just ten minutes earlier was sitting under a cow. Don't worry; he usually washed before milking. He would then go through a thorough process of preparing the milk for drinking. He would strain it through a piece of cheesecloth and put it in the icebox. That was it.

This was the morning routine every single day of the week. Most of those days I was the last out of bed, but once in a while I would get up and trail along with Daddy Freeman while he worked. One particular morning we had fed everything, and we headed to the barn to milk the cow. When I say "we," I mean Daddy Freeman. He talked me into trying my hand, so to speak, at milking once, but it was just too much for this city boy. Anyway, we opened the door to the barn, and lying inside was the milk cow, which seemed to me to have parts in places that didn't belong. Before my eyes could adjust to the light and get a good look, Daddy Freeman had whisked me back outside, and he had disappeared into the barn. His "Stay here" was said in such a way that I would still be there today if he hadn't reappeared some time later and invited me in. I ventured in, cautiously. Inside was one of the most unbelievable sights of my life. There wasn't just one cow in the barn; somehow there were now two. Wobbling before me was a halfway spread-eagle calf that had appeared from, well, I didn't know where it had come from. It certainly wasn't there before, not yesterday, not that morning. It was a miracle.

There is a word in Hebrew (*bara*) that we translate as "create." It is only used with "God" as the subject. No exceptions. How God creates is the topic of thousands upon thousands of textbooks around the world. All faiths and cultures have their take on it. Six days or six million-plus years? Create out of nothing or create from something? One man, one woman, or one humanity? Your opinion is as good as the next. None of that mattered to that little wide-eyed boy standing in the barn on a foggy summer morning. He was forming perhaps his first understanding about God. It wasn't there, and then it was. It was a miracle. Still is today.

*God saw everything that he had made, and indeed, it was very good.* — Genesis 1:31

# I Hear That Train a-Rollin'

Mama Bea and Daddy Freeman rarely left the farm at Shake Rag. Daddy Freeman went into Okolona about once a week to buy things like sugar and flour. He always took about six dozen eggs to sell while he was there. I think they went for about fifty cents a dozen. He would always stop at my Uncle Heard's car dealership to visit and sometimes pick up a check. He worked for Uncle Heard for a while to help make ends meet. I'm not sure what he did. I suppose he worked on cars, but if he worked on cars like he did tillers, well, that's another story.

On occasion Mama Bea and Daddy Freeman did come to our house at 922 Franklin Street in Grenada, Mississippi. Usually it would be special occasions like Christmas or Thanksgiving. I never did like that. I always preferred going to Shake Rag for such things because it gave me a chance to chase chickens and hunt. I guess their coming to Grenada was Mom's way of taking some of the work off of Mama Bea. Now, Grenada was not a booming metropolis, but it was huge compared to Shake Rag and was even bigger than Okolona. Some of Grenada's size could be attributed to the lake that it was near, but probably the railroad was a major factor in its growth. The Illinois Central Railroad was in Grenada, and its track ran right behind our house. My dad worked for the railroad as well as his brother, Uncle Charlie. Uncle Charlie was a conductor, and I often ran outside to wave at him as he passed by on the train's caboose. But I digress.

Mama Bea and Daddy Freeman's first visit to 922 Franklin came right after my parents had bought the house and had moved in with their newborn son (that would be me). Now as long as I can remember, I don't think I ever heard a train pass by our house at night while we were sleeping. It's not that they didn't come by; I just never heard it, not in my almost eighteen years of living there. That was not the case for my grandparents. Coming from Shake Rag, the loudest noise they ever heard at night was a hoot owl. That is, if you don't count the shotgun blast in the direction of a turkey thief one night, but that also is another story. Well, it was summer, and the windows were wide open. All was quiet when out of the darkness came this earth-shaking, glass-shattering blast of a train whistle followed by a rumble on the tracks that can only be described as apocalyptic. I never heard it. Mom and Dad didn't hear it. But Mama Bea and Daddy Freeman heard it, and I'm quite certain that after they stopped levitating over the bed, they vowed to never leave Shake Rag again, at least not to come to 922 Franklin Street for an overnight visit.

Strange, isn't it? That everyday occurrence of a train's whistle and the thunder of rolling down the tracks, practically in my backyard, was barely ever noticed. We always slept soundly. I guess we were used to it. The cacophony of sound became barely more than a whisper to our ears.

Strange too is that God, every day, comes to us in innumerable ways and we miss it. God goes unnoticed, despite his sometimes thundering presence. We have become desensitized. We are unaware because we are so accustomed to his leaning in toward us that it is little more than a mere nicety along our path. The song of the mockingbird. The fragrance of the rose. The laughter of a child. The kind gesture of a stranger. The nudging of memories. The stories of the elderly. The joys of life and the grace to live through the pain. God's presence.

Look for it.

Today.

Every day.

# I Hate

I hate drugs. The illegal kind. I hate that people's lives are so crappy that they turn to drugs. I hate that the systems that are created to help, hurt. I hate poverty. I hate the powers of our culture and world that propagate poverty. I hate the devaluation of parenthood and its responsibilities. I hate a culture that gives permission to those who have children to leave them. I hate that people are hungry. I hate that in the most agriculturally productive country in the world that people have to eat out of the back of a "food truck" or garbage bins. I hate war. I hate that it kills people. I hate that it destroys. I hate that it robs resources that should or could be used to feed and educate. War diverts resources that could provide medicine and counseling to the mentally disabled who are among those eating from garbage bins. I hate prisons. I hate that we store people like cattle in a place that oftentimes only serves to mutate people or perpetuate the very reasons that they are there.

I hate loneliness. I hate that senior adults sit quietly in their homes, the last of their family, with children who have abandoned them. Sitting there staring at a plate with no one to share their life, no one to have a conversation with, no one. I hate that their wisdom is relegated to outdated information or dusty archives that exist but are never accessed. I hate bigotry. I hate that there are people who think they are better than "them." Those who do, aren't. I hate disease that infiltrates bones and brains, livers, and lymph nodes, debilitating, devouring, ending. I hate abortion. More specifically, I hate the need for abortion. There are so many childless couples who grieve monthly when the little stick doesn't change colors, so many teens whose lives are forever changed. I hate autism, from Asperger's all the way across to the other side, whatever or wherever that is. Loving and lovable children, bright and energetic children, some content and some tortured, but all categorized and labeled, even segregated.

I hate that complete strangers are called to a hospital nursery to pick up a baby to take home and love because there are no parents who can. I hate that eleven months later that child will, through her heart and eyes, forever lose the only parents she knew existed. Abandoned.

I hate that a man offered a way of life that seeks justice and peace and love and then was killed. I hate that people claim to follow those teachings but offer little evidence of such a life. I hate that poverty and war and bigotry can be ended, can be stopped, can be eradicated, but those who follow don't, not really. I hate that I don't follow enough. I don't stand up and stand in enough. I hate that my fears drive me to ignore and disregard, to relegate and to dismiss words, life-changing, systems-changing words. I hate that I don't let a Savior save me, all of me: my thoughts, my actions, my heart, my relationships, my time, my devotion, my, my, my…I hate that I'm so arrogant that I think in terms of "my" when it is not mine. It is the Savior's.

I am told there will be a time when there will be no war. There will be a time when this earth will become new, again, for the third and final time. I am told that enemies will be no more and love will rule the day — that day. I long for that day. I hope for that day. It is not now. The kingdom is present but not nearly enough. So we wait and wait. The procession of a king arrives this Sunday. A day we remember when a few gathered to receive him while on the other side of town the throngs rallied to receive the kingdom of Caesar's power. Nothing much has changed. But it must, change, that is. The world needs to change. I need to change. We need, no, I need a renewal. Maybe even…a resurrection.

# House Fire

These cold temperatures remind of winter nights in Shake Rag. Every night before bed Daddy Freeman would turn the heat off in the house. By morning the house would be frigid, and even getting one of my toes to be willing to peek out from under the massive covers was a chore. Most mornings Daddy Freeman got out of bed before me, so the house would be well on its way to a reasonable temperature by the time Mama Bea's biscuits came out of the oven.

The habit of turning the heat off in the house got Daddy Freeman into some serious trouble one day. This happened well before I came along, so I only know the story from my Uncle Fred. By the time I made it into the world, Mama Bea and Daddy Freeman lived in a small cinder-block house that was built on a slab. It basically had a living room, a combination dining room and kitchen, two bedrooms, and one bath. Before this house they had what I suppose was a typical farmhouse. I've only seen one corner of the house in an old black and white photograph. It looked to be a white clapboard house with a front porch. The house was built on what we call today as pier and beam. That just means you could crawl under it. My mother used to hide her little brother (Uncle Fred) under the house when Daddy Freeman was looking for him to help him learn a lesson, if you know what I mean.

Insulation hadn't been invented yet, and on a particularly cold winter day, the pipes froze. Now this wasn't anything unusual, and Daddy Freeman had a fix for it. In fact, Daddy Freeman had a fix for about everything that broke. You will remember the stubborn garden tiller and his favorite tool, a hammer. And I'm pretty sure that his tractor had more baling wire in the motor than actual tractor parts. Anyway, Daddy Freeman rolled up some newspapers and crawled under the house to get to the exposed, frozen pipes. No doubt he had done this every winter, maybe even several times each year. He lit the newspaper and held it up to the pipes to thaw them. Maybe it was so cold that he was shaking and couldn't keep the torch steady. Maybe he got distracted looking at the wiring. Maybe he had just come home from one of his weekend misadventures and was still enjoying the residual effects. Whatever the reason, that old pine flooring that was as dry as the hay in the barn suddenly caught fire. You can see it. He probably first tried to blow it out. Then maybe he took off his old felt hat and began beating it. Pretty soon it was just too much. By the time he had crawled out, the house was an inferno. Mama Bea was dragged from the house. On her way out she had the presence of mind to reach and grab a photograph, the only thing in the entire house that was saved, besides Mama Bea, of course.

They built the cinder-block house almost in the exact same spot as the first. Mama Bea had them turn the house slightly away from the road. She was convinced that it would help keep the dust down. It didn't. Life continued, and as far as I ever knew, they were happy with the new place. Neither of the houses was a mansion. By every financial standard Freeman and Bera Ogg were poor. Uncle Fred says they were poorer than poor. They got by with what they had (and didn't have). They didn't need a lot of stuff, and what they had, well, what they had was enough. What they did have plenty of was honesty, generous hearts, loyal friends and family: brothers and sisters, children and grandchildren who have made this world better.

We are told that there are mansions that await us when we get to heaven. Mama Bea got there before Daddy Freeman. When he arrived, I suspect he found that Mama Bea hadn't really been too concerned with how big theirs was as long as the pipes didn't freeze. They probably aren't poor now either. Come to think of it, they weren't poor when they were here. Freeman and Bera Ogg were wealthy. Even when all they had was a single photograph grabbed from a burning house.

*...I have learned to be content with whatever I have.* — Philippians 4:11

# Here, Chick, Chick

There were three buildings on Mama Bea and Daddy Freeman's place in Shake Rag. There was the house. It was a four-room, cinder-block house that had been built to replace their original house. Their original house was made of wood and burned to the ground when Daddy Freeman crawled under it with a fiery ball of newspapers that he was using to thaw the pipes. Oops.

Like any farm, they also had a barn. It wasn't much to look at. It was made of old tin that had been nailed to some even older posts. It was where the hay was stored, where the milking was done, and where the pigs came in from the cold in the winter. The floor was straw-covered dirt, along with a few things the cows left behind. That old barn was blown down by a big storm, and Daddy Freeman built a bigger, better barn. I like to think that I helped build it. I think I handed him one piece of tin and then went off to fish.

Then there was the combination smokehouse and henhouse. The two rooms, if you will, were separated by a common wall. On the smokehouse side there were a couple saddles, the collar and reigns for the mule, the corn for the chickens, and a few tools. At the back of this small space was a rough table that was covered with about two inches of salt. Above it were the nails that were used to hold the hams that hung there, cured with salt.

On the henhouse side there were about twenty or so nesting boxes for the hens. Overhead there were some poles for the chickens to roost on. It was in the boxes that the hens laid their eggs and from which they were gathered every morning. I had a love/hate feeling about the chore. While I loved being trusted to gather the delicate treasures that the hens left, I hated going into the henhouse. The smell was terrible, and the hens, well, they were downright scary. Glaring at you with those beady eyes, wondering what right you had to be invading and stealing from them. And those beaks looked lethal. One time, and only one time, my mischievous grandfather told me to put my hand under the hen that was still in the box to see if there were any eggs. Daddy Freeman didn't bother telling me that the old hen was setting (waiting on chicks to hatch). Besides, I had already seen him slip his hand under two other hens just a box or two over. The hens just watched as he gently slipped his hand under them, raised them up, and after checking the eggs, put the hens back down. So not having learned my lesson from other times I saw that smirk on Daddy Freeman's face, I slowly moved my hand toward the hen. Those old demonic beady eyes followed every inch of the way. PECK, PECK, PECK with jackhammer quickness and force came that beak down onto my hand with a precision that could be measured in micrometers. Searing pain raced up my arm, and I quickly checked to see if one of my fingers had gone the way of one of the many worms I had seen chickens pulling from the ground: 1, 2, 3, 4, 5. All there. I turned to look at Daddy Freeman only to see the familiar grin that always followed such lessons.

This stranger wasn't about to get close to those soon-to-be chicks. But Daddy Freeman was different. Those old, rough, sun-baked hands were familiar. They had held every egg and guarded every chick that had hatched there on the farm. Even the hen that was setting that day had probably seen Daddy Freeman before it had even seen the sun. His voice had called them to breakfast every day of their entire lives. "Heeerrrrre, chick, chick, chick," he would call as he scattered corn out into the yard. He was familiar, well known, trusted.

There is one who knows us, knows our heart, knows our mind, knows everything about us. He was present at birth and has been all the days of our lives. He has suffered with us during our illnesses and the dark days that life brings. He has celebrated the birth of our children, our retirements, our gains at work and school. He knows us. He has cried tears of joy when we received him as our own and tears of sadness when we turned aside for selfish goals. He knows us. He has lifted us in our despair, lovingly nurtured our souls in solitude. He gifts us with the spirit of comfort in our grief, whether it be over our first pet goldfish or our closest friend. He knows us. Our burdens are his. Our joys he shares. He has counted our tears and keeps them in a bottle. Peace and grace are ours because he desires it to be so. He calls our names and beckons us to come to him, come to him as a deer to fresh springs. Come to him to find what the heart longs for and the soul needs. He calls our names. He knows us. He is Jesus, and he died for us.

*He calls his own sheep by name and leads them out. When he has brought out all his own, he goes ahead of them, and the sheep follow him because they know his voice. They will not follow a stranger.... I came that they may have life, and have it abundantly.* — John 10:3-5, 10

# Hammer Time

Mama Bea and Daddy Freeman had a huge garden every summer. All kinds of vegetables were raised, picked, pickled, and then frozen or canned, which is a funny way to say they were put in jars. They were both hard workers, and I'll always believe that their work ethic kept them healthy. That said, when the heat of mid-summer came, despite their predisposition to hard work, they tended to rest around noon for a couple hours or so. Lunch, a bottle of Coke, *As the World Turns*, and a nap in the recliners helped rejuvenate them for the afternoon of work.

I vividly remember one particular day that Daddy Freeman's midday siesta was stretching a bit long. "Freeman, the garden needs to be tilled." No response. "FREEMAN!" That was enough, and out of the chair he went. Now, I wouldn't say that Mama Bea wore the pants in the family, but she definitely washed, starched, and ironed them, and Daddy Freeman knew if he didn't get going, there wouldn't be any pants for anyone to wear. So up and out of the recliner went Daddy Freeman, and as he marched down to the garden, with me trailing a safe five steps behind, I could hear something along the lines of, "That woman #%&** can't rest *+=#%^ work is all @!!!!&%."

The tiller was an old machine that was held together with baling wire and Daddy Freeman's sweat and spit (baling wire is what bales of hay used to be bound with). He checked the gas, set the choke, and gave the old gal a strong pull to start the engine. Cough. Spit. Chug. He pulled again…and again…and again. Nothing. Daddy Freeman went up to where he kept his tools, which were in the trunk of something like a 1932 Pontiac that had found its final resting place next to the smokehouse, which was next to the chicken house. Back he came. He pulled out the spark plug and cleaned it, adjusted some screws that I'm sure were important, and pulled the starter rope again…and again…and again. Mama Bea's name was then invoked with less than romantic tones, and then he reached for it. The "it" was his hammer. I found this a bit unusual and wondered what he was going to do. I found out. He took that hammer and raised it high over his head. Wham! Wham! Wham! Right on top of the tiller, the hammer found its mark. I took a step back, wondering what would happen if I didn't start when Daddy Freeman wanted me to. He then grabbed the rope, pulled hard, and the, tiller realizing it was overmatched, started right up.

Aren't we glad that God doesn't have a hammer? Some would argue that. Some would say that bad things happen to us because God wants to get our attention. Some would say that God punishes us for our misdeeds and allows our car to run into a tree or for our bodies to succumb to some horrible disease. Surely God is not vindictive. Surely God does not return evil for evil. Surely God is different than our models of justice.

God is good and desires our good. God loves us and does not desire that any be punished but that all live life joyously and in the abundance of his grace. Bad things happen. There is no doubt about that, and some of those bad things are natural consequences to our bad choices. Some just happen. But God is not the initiator of those bad things, nor does he simply allow them. God does what God can, for us, for his creation, for his kingdom. We are not tillers that just need a little corrosion knocked off of us. We are the beloved, God's good creation, chosen, redeemed, Spirit-filled, the body of Christ, and God loves us. Hammer time? Not with God.

Grace. Only grace. Always grace.

# Green Grass

I returned to work today after five days of being very, very sick. It is good to be back and out in the sunshine. As my senior adult friends say, "It's a good day when you can see the green grass." Now, the grass isn't green this time of year, so I assume that seeing the green grass means you aren't under the grass. It also happens to be my birthday, and being able to see another year click by is always good, especially at fifty-three.

As I lay there in bed over the last several days, there were many thoughts and questions that came to mind:
- "Do they make caskets for men who are 6'5"?"
- "Why does Jana have the life insurance policy out?"
- "It's 4:00 A.M., and the Australian Open is on. Do tennis balls fall up 'Down Under'?"
- "I wonder if that spider on the ceiling is as sick as I am. I hope so."
- "It's been ten days; maybe they will find one more survivor in Haiti."
- "How can so many ever find hope in the midst of such devastation?"
- "How does my friend with pancreatic cancer get out of bed every day?"
- "The death of a child is not just the loss of a life; it is the death of your life."
- "Can people who experience such suffering ever see green grass again?"

My duel with the flu was temporarily debilitating. But it was temporary, and today life is good again, just after a few days of illness. Not so for others. The pain continues, and the battles are waged with a ferocity that most of us can hardly comprehend. Picking through rubble in Haiti. Another blood test. Another pill. Another day of grief.

This week, do your part as the body of Christ and help care for its members. Offer a word of grace to those you know who suffer, every day. Still more importantly, pray for them and let them know you did so. Not to show yourself to be a pious person, but to show the other that their burden is shared. It will offer some relief to the load they bear, and perhaps, just perhaps, their grass will be a little greener for it.

# God's Cheers

Go Zackary. Go Zackary. Go Zackary. Go Zackary. Come to McGucken Park most any Tuesday evening these days, and you'll see a crazed bald guy standing on the sideline of a soccer game yelling his lungs out. Go Zackary. And go he does. He's a fleet-footed little guy. Zackary hangs back from the wad of players competing for control of the ball until it eventually pops out. Zackary is there waiting. His coach says he is a strategically smart player. I think he looks at those flying feet and trembles. Anyway, he gets the ball and streaks toward the goal with the bald guy encouraging every step. Go Zackary. Inevitably, he gets to the goal and loses control, sending the ball to unpredictable places.

My heart sinks. I want him to score. I want him to be successful. So I yell some more. Then the coach yells. Then the players yell. So why is Zackary smiling with all this yelling going on? Because everybody is yelling, "Way to go, Zackary!" "Good playing, Zackary!" "Great shot, Zackary!" We celebrate the good that he did without dwelling on the mistake.

Don't you wish our adult life was more like that. We make mistakes, and more often than not we hear the stinging words of blame. Accusations fly, and insults are muttered. "Fire the coach." "She did that on purpose." "He knew better." Worst of all are our own condemning words. We are indeed our own worst judge. Recordings from years ago start playing in our heads that we aren't valuable. We can't succeed. We deserved what we got.

Thankfully, God is not like that. God is always with us, cheering us on, "Go, Howard. Go, Mary. Go, Steve. You can do it." God desires our best, always. Mistakes? I make them. You make them. But God says to us, "You are forgiven." Others may condemn. We may condemn ourselves. But we have a "cheerleader" that is always, always cheering us on. Go, Terri. Go, Mike. Go, Jane. Way to go!

*If God is for us, who is against us?* — Romans 8:31

# Hell's Fire

Daddy Freeman wasn't a religious man, at least from what I could tell. It seemed we spent more Sunday mornings hunting or fishing than in the church house. I do remember him invoking God's name a time or two, though. There is the story of when the pastor came to visit. He and Mama Bea were still living in the old farmhouse that eventually burned to the ground. The preacher was there on a hot summer day, probably making the rounds in Shake Rag to the backsliders, of which I suspect Daddy Freeman to have been one. The old house had plank floors that covered a crawlspace underneath. It was a good place to keep things cool on hot days. In this case it was Daddy Freeman's home brew. As the temperature rose, so did the contents of bottle upon bottle of his hidden elixir. The caps on those old bottles did what they could, but eventually they had to let go under the pressure that was mounting in each bottle. First one went off, and POW! — it hit those wood floors and made the sound of a rifle going off. Then there was the second. Blam! Then the third and fourth, and suddenly it was as if the second battalion had cut loose on the enemy, all from those popping bottles and rocketing caps banging up against the old wooden planks. That's as far as this story ever got in its telling at family reunions. My guess is that Daddy Freeman was more grieved that he had lost his brew than that the preacher had been the beneficiary of the surprise.

There was one other time that Daddy Freeman's religion surfaced. It too was associated with grief. I must have been about ten or twelve years old. A piece of land had been cleared to make more pasture. I didn't like it, the clearing, that is. The small patch of woods was always occupied by a squirrel or two and at least one rabbit. That, despite my best efforts to invite them to dinner and Mama Bea's frying pan. When the land had been cleared, the larger trees were pushed up into a giant pile to be burned. Inside the pile were old tires, fuel for the ensuing inferno. Daddy Freeman climbed over into the pile and lit a starter fire. Soon the tires were burning and the fire was spreading. The fire was so hot that the flames were blue. As we stood there, my grandfather fixed his gaze upon the blue flames and said with seemingly a bit of grief, "The fires of hell are ten times hotter." We stood there a while longer, just watching in silence.

His words have haunted me. I have never known if Daddy Freeman was contemplating his own future or pondering the destination of so many who had gone before him. Maybe it was even a word of warning to this preteen. I'll have to admit that it stuck. Hell was very real to him. It's not so much anymore, at least among the "educated." We don't think as much about a place or fire as much as about the sheer agony of not being with God. I think we should be as focused on the present as much as on the future. "Hell on earth," as the expression goes, is far more real to me. The abused and neglected children who pass through my home render any speculation about hell that one might have to nothingness. We are far from "Thy Kingdom come." Maybe we would all do well to pause and ponder the future of those we love and don't love. Maybe God would be just as pleased if we would spend some time pondering the fate of so many innocent sufferers of greed, war, and a host of other evils who live happily in that blue flame of unjust existence.

# Fire Ants

There weren't many dangers at Mama Bea and Daddy Freeman's farm in Shake Rag. There weren't any bears or cougars, at least outside of a little boy's imagination. Probably the most prevalent and hated dangerous critter was the cotton-mouth moccasin, like the one that bit Mama Bea in the strawberry patch. Daddy Freeman probably manufactured more dangerous situations than what actually existed. Like the time he had me stick my hand down into a paper sack to guess what was in it. Turns out it was a snapping turtle that grabbed my finger and wouldn't let go. Ouch! Then there was the time he wanted me to ride a horse he had raised from a colt. As we were trying to catch him to put a saddle and bridle on, he busted through two 2x6 planks and ran straight through a four-strand barbed-wire fence. That was the end of that, and I'm still quite certain my grandfather loved me, I think.

By and large, the forty-eight-acre farm was a safe place for the meanderings of a little boy. However, there was one critter that caused grown men to cry. They had invaded our country from the West and were inching their way across the South. It was the fire ant. Most of us today know about fire ants, but forty years ago they were rather new to the South. These little industrious insects would build mounds that dotted the pasture and gave fair warning to the cattle and kids that they were not to be messed with. For me, the mounds were invitations to wreak havoc upon these demon-possessed creatures. A long stick jammed into the heart of mound as if slaying a dragon brought ants streaming out in search of the invader. A few seconds of delight, and off I'd be in search of the next beacon of terror.

One day I was fishing. Concentrating on the fine art of casting my purple worm, I hadn't noticed that uninvited guests had arrived. It seems that fire ants have a way to subdue even the largest of their enemies. They, by the hundreds, will cover their victims and then, with a single signal from their blood-thirsty leader, chomp down all at the same time. And they did. There is a very practical reason they are called fire ants. Fire literally began with my toes and seared its way up my legs to my knees. My screams offered no relief, and I couldn't wipe the beasts off fast enough, so I decided to fight fire with water. With one great leap, I was in the pond. The damage was done, though. I came out of the water and found my legs covered in dime-sized whelps. First there was pain, then itching, and then for the rest of my life the memory and the hatred — no, loathing —

of those mean, deceitful, terrorizing, murderous, acidic, vile enemies of all that is right and good in the world.

Like the fire ant mounds that dot the pasture, it is sometimes easy to spot our enemies. They are the murderers, the rapists, and the terrorists that riddle our newspapers every day. They are easy to hate, and we do, because forgiving them of such heinous behavior is crazy. Besides, it's hard work to forgive. By in large they are faceless individuals or groups that we will never know personally, so it is easier to relegate them to the hate column and save our forgiving for others. But even then, it becomes difficult. There are those folks closer to home who are our enemies. Maybe enemy is too strong for some of them. They just plain get under our skin. They are co-workers, in-laws, neighbors, and others who seem to take some bit of delight in making our lives miserable. They, like the ants, make their way into our space and then "chomp." Damage is done. Forgiveness? We forgave them last week and the week before. That's plenty, don't you think?

Maybe those misguided words from a brother or spouse should not even be mentioned. It's easier to overlook and forget, or at least try to forget, than it is to forgive. After all, why open the proverbial can of worms? We have a lifetime to live together, and, well, it's just easier.

Of course, we know what Jesus said. Forgive seventy-seven times. Forgive as we are forgiven. Forgive; they don't know what they are doing. All that stuff. It is stuff that takes hard work, tenacity, intentionality, patience, and love. Oh yeah, "love," as in "love your enemies."

Surely he didn't mean the fire ants.

# Elliott and Lonnie

Elliott was a black man who worked for Daddy Freeman on the farm in Shake Rag. It is a real reach for me to even remember his name. I was a small boy when Elliott would come across the road from his shotgun shack to plow the cottonfield out in front of Mama Bea and Daddy Freeman's house. Elliott would harness up the mule and could plow a row as straight as any John Deere can today. I remember the "Gee" and the "Haw" as Elliott would direct the old mule down the row and then make the turn to come back. The sun was hot and quickly baked the fresh dirt that peeled back under the push of the steel blade, my feet struggling to keep their balance on these earthen boulders. I loved it.

Elliott was married to Lonnie. Again, my memory lacks clarity, but what remains stirs feelings of friendship for her. I can remember following behind her after the cotton had burst open, making the front pasture look like a ski slope in Colorado. Dragging her big, heavy bag along, she quickly and nimbly would pull the white gold from its prickly home and stow it away in the big bag. I would try, but after a while the stings were too much for me, so I would go jump in the cotton that was loaded on the old wooden trailer.

This was the 1960s, and things were changing. Shake Rag had gone untouched by the social melee until one day when things got a little out of kilter. For however long that Elliott and Lonnie had worked for my grandparents, they had been satisfied with hand-me-down clothes, canned goods, and other things as payment for their work. Then, one day, Lonnie said, "No, thanks." Mama Bea was appalled. She didn't want the clothes? As I recall, there was a reference to someone being "uppity" now. My foggy memory tells me that over the next weeks and months, we didn't see Elliott and Lonnie that much. Then they are gone from my memory altogether. I don't know if they moved or just stopped working for my grandparents. Their old shack stood on the hill across the road for a long time. I suppose it is still there.

Mama Bea, Daddy Freeman, Elliott, and Lonnie had been friends. There was mutual care and respect. The symbiotic friendship that had worked well for so many years had now changed forever. What happened there on the farm in Shake Rag was just a glimmer of what was taking place across the South and the nation. A ray of light was beginning to shine through the darkness. Laws were changing. Attitudes were changing. Relationships were changing.

Fast-forward to 2010 to this proud descendant of Shake Rag, the Sullivans, and the Oggs. I have in my home an infant who is African American. She is a foster child, whom we will love for a few months, and then she will be on her way. Last weekend, three strapping young men came to visit my daughter and her friend in our home. They were African Americans, and they were received like any other boys, with a welcoming smile and a cautious eye; after all, they are teenage boys.

I wonder what Mama Bea would think. I wonder what Lonnie would think. It is certain to me that today they have clarity about such things that were impossible when they were with us. They have been received into the arms of the one whose light continues to change us and the world. Maybe one day we will get it right. Maybe one day God's good creation will allow enough light in so that injustice is no longer the norm. Race won't be an issue. Gender won't be an issue. The weak will be empowered, and the hungry will be fed. Maybe one day life will be able to plow a row that is as straight as Elliott's and our sin will be as white as the cottonfields of Shake Rag.

*I am the light of the world.* — John 8:12

# Eggs to Ashes

Early in my work as a minister, I was asked by the church to serve as interim pastor. The former pastor had been absconded by a church in Texas, and the church called on me to fill the void while they searched for a replacement. I was honored. It turned out to be the most unusual year of the twenty-four-plus years that I have served churches.

John called the church one afternoon in August. He began by telling me that his father had been kidnapped. What followed was a story that could have been torn from a Hollywood script. Bill had been trying to sell his Corvette and was at home when a knock came at the door. A couple guys were interested in the car. As Bill was showing them the vintage vehicle, one of the men pulled a pistol, forced Bill into the trunk of the Corvette, and the two began driving around Jackson, Mississippi. Bill was a big man who probably weighed close to 275 pounds. You can only imagine what it was like to be stuffed into the very small trunk of a Corvette and driven around for hours in the heat of an exhaustingly hot August day in Mississippi. To make a bad situation absolutely horrendous, the two began firing the pistol through the backseat and into the trunk. Bill was shot several times.

The two finally stopped the Corvette at a convenience store. While the car was parked, Bill managed to pop open the trunk and stagger across the street to a pay phone. He dialed 911 and was soon rescued and taken to the hospital, where he was in the ICU for several days. Bill died by the end of the week. John asked me to do the funeral.

Bill was a rugged sort of man who lived life on the edges. He had a passion for fast cars and fast airplanes. It was only natural that Bill's ashes would be scattered across a grass airstrip just outside of Jackson. Family and friends gathered at the funeral home, where I gave a eulogy. It was maybe my second or third funeral, and I had never met Bill, so to say I was nervous would have been an understatement. Somehow I muddled through, and the family seemed sincerely pleased. We got into our cars for the procession and headed north to the airstrip.

When we arrived, I slipped back into my black robe and carefully placed the white stole about my neck. The humidity, temperature, and glaring sun caused beads of sweat to form on my face immediately. The family also felt the heaviness of the air as they sat in metal folding chairs along the edge of the runway. There was to be a flyover with a missing pilot, which would be followed by a single-engine plane from which the ashes would be distributed. I got this information from a rather stern-looking woman who held a two-way radio. When I inquired about the direction of the plane, she quickly reminded me that I was just the minister and that she was in charge. She scared me, so I responded with a quiet, "Yes, ma'am." I did manage to request a prayer between the missing pilot flyover and the dispersing of the ashes, which was granted.

We all waited. Sweating. I kept a close eye on the family, worried that someone might succumb to the heat. I kept a closer eye on the woman with the radio. She scared me. Then, on cue, the three planes with the open space for the missing pilot came over. It was a memorable moment. I quickly prayed something about "ashes to ashes" and "grace" and more stuff. We waited, again. Soon the sputter of an engine could be heard in the distance. The small plane came up the airstrip and made a hard left turn in front of the family. A hand and container popped out, and then there was a puff of gray by the plane. I looked over at the woman in charge, and she seemed quite pleased with herself. I, however, knew things were about to get, um, messy. Soon, family members were quietly brushing their dark suits and dresses. They were wiping their foreheads and noses. My black robe was now covered in white flecks. You guessed it. The more we wiped our faces, the worse it got. We looked like a bunch of Catholics with an overzealous priest coming out of church on Ash Wednesday.

No one said a word, not a word. They filed by me, offering their hands in gratitude, and we all went home. The woman in charge was quiet now, not even offering a glance my way. Who could blame her? After all, I was just a minister who happened to wonder about the plane's direction.

Now, if you have had a little chuckle over this story, don't be ashamed. I thought you would. It has been my hope that when the family got some separation from the loss, they were able to smile, if not even belly laugh over the miscue. Certainly God gets a laugh now and then over humanity's foibles.

So today and this week, as you go about your routine and you make a miscalculation and wind up with egg on your face, pause and smile with God. After all, it could be worse.

# Deliver Me from Evil

When I was thirteen years old, I was as tall as I am now. My long legs were a nuisance to my mother, who had the unenviable task of locating blue jeans that had a twenty-eight-inch waist and an inseam of thirty-six inches. Despite the pain in finding suitable dungarees to cover my wiry frame, my long legs came in handy. I could easily change a light bulb and could mow the yard in about half the time as my shorter friends. They were also useful in Shake Rag.

Somehow, Daddy Freeman acquired a pony. Not a horse, but a pony. It wasn't the friendliest of ponies. It rarely came right up to you unless you had a handful of corn or sugar. Then it was a brave soul who allowed those huge teeth to nip away at the palm of your hand. It didn't like bridles, and it didn't like saddles. It could be tricked into getting the bridle on if you were willing to lose a finger with those nipping teeth. Without a saddle, it was a formidable ride. However, that's where my long legs came in. Despite its huge belly, I could practically wrap my legs around its midsection, and off we would go with the bitter weed slapping at my toes. There were times I wasn't sure which one of us was in control, often going left when I was quite certain I had pulled to the right. But we had fun. At least I did. I'm not so sure about the pony.

At some point Daddy Freeman decided to breed the pony with a horse. Not a pony, but a horse. The result was a horse. Not a big horse, but it definitely was bigger than its mama, and so was its attitude. This thing did not like saddles, bridles, sugar, corn, or people, as far as I could tell. Daddy Freeman decided it was time to break the horse, and he decided his long-legged city grandson was the one to do it. He wouldn't let me drive the tractor but he would put me on the steed from, well, you know. We finally got the horse-zilla into the lot by the barn. We worked until we got him cornered next to the cattle ramp. The cattle ramp inclined up to about three or four feet so that cattle could be loaded into a truck to be taken to auction. Across the upper end of the cattle ramp were two 2x6 planks. They were there to keep the cattle from falling off and hurting themselves.

So there we were, Daddy Freeman, me, and the horse. The horse looked at us and then looked at the cattle ramp. Daddy Freeman was determined. So was the horse. I was praying. Daddy Freeman wasn't budging, and the horse figured that out and took off up the cattle ramp. Without hesitating he jumped through the 2x6 boards, landed with hooves of lightning, ran through a four-strand barbed-wire fence, and victoriously took a lap around the pasture. I told Daddy Freeman that I would never ride that horse. He offered that mischievous grin of his and nodded his head. He understood.

In that event there was a cauldron of emotions inside me, most of which were fear. The mere thought of my hefting myself atop of that evil critter made me wonder if I would live to see another day. I couldn't let it show, though. I had to prove to Daddy Freeman that this city boy was up to the challenge. Then there was immense relief and thanksgiving as the horse pranced defiantly around the pasture. I may have even felt a kinship, blood brothers of sorts. We were both free!

That cauldron bubbled again this past week as I talked with a doctor about my "condition." Back home they might call it "low blood." The doctor said my platelets were dangerously low and my white count didn't fare much better. Fear crept in. No, that's not true. It pranced boldly in. She explained the possible causes, some not so bad, some not so good. She said be careful. Don't play basketball, don't climb ladders, and don't bump your head. Go to the ER if you do. I found myself eye to eye with another evil critter and praying again, being fearful again, not wanting to be where I was. My long legs won't help me with this one. This time the emotions showed, and I spent some bit of time mopping my cheeks. I didn't have Daddy Freeman to stare down the creature, so I called a couple church folk. They gladly took on the job of praying for me. Others know now, and they are praying too. By the end of this month, I'll know more. In the meantime, the love of family and friends sustains me as I wait.

I confess I don't know how prayer works, not really. But I believe in it. I don't think my praying at the bottom of that cattle ramp caused that horse to fly. But I do believe prayer offers strength, patience, the grace to be thankful, and sometimes healing comes, even in the face of the worst of times. Some of you have already experienced all of that.

So I'll be praying that this new critter from the depths will also take a flying leap. And I'll wait. We'll wait. Maybe I'll change a few light bulbs.

*Perfect love casts out fear.* — 1 John 4:18

# Bogue Creek

When I was twelve years old, I had an unusual assortment of friends: Jerry, Gary, and Snake Doctor. Jerry lived down the street and across the sewage ditch. The ditch was a dividing line between the haves and the have-nots. Jerry was on the have-nots side. His four-room shack had a living room, a bedroom, a kitchen, and a bathroom that didn't have a shower or tub. We called them shotgun shacks because, as you know, a shotgun could be fired in the front door and the shot would go out the back without hitting the walls. Jerry was a relatively nice kid, as was Gary, his cousin. Snake Doctor was from a similar background as Jerry but wasn't all that nice. Actually, he was a little bit scary and unpredictable. All of them were three years older than I was.

One day we all decided to make a trip to Bogue Creek. This meant sneaking off from home for me. Jerry, Gary, and Snake Doctor didn't have to sneak because their parents didn't care where they were, ever. Jerry grabbed his 410 shotgun, and off we went. We crossed the railroad tracks, the "black" cemetery, and meandered our way through a stand of trees to the creek. We had made the trip many times. On this trip we decided to shoot shad, little silvery fish that swim in schools. We were having a grand time shooting at the fish and watching them blast out of the water.

At some point Jerry made his way out onto a sand bar, and I stood on the bank near him. The school of fish darted into the water that separated the bank from the sand bar. Now, even a twelve-year-old knows a little bit about angles and a phenomenon called ricochet, so when Jerry raised the shotgun, I threw my arms up in front of my face and screamed, "No!" Too late. My legs were on fire. I looked down, and there were little holes in my pants' legs. I quickly pulled them up to find dozens of little bits of lead buried in my very skinny legs. There was also blood. Not much, but enough to scare me, Jerry, Gary, and even tough guy Snake Doctor, who I was sure had shot a few people already, on purpose. We sat there on the bank picking the shot out and blotting the blood with my pants. Not being mortally wounded, we headed back home. When I got home, I yelled to Mom that I was back and dashed to my room. I quickly changed pants and stuffed my bloodied pants into a paper bag that I snuck into the trashcan out back. Safe! I didn't wear shorts for a couple weeks while my wounds healed. Mom never asked about the missing pants. All was well at home, and the shad were able to live their lives out peacefully because of a lesson learned.

Thirty years later the phone rang. It was Dad with his weekly Saturday morning call. After we had discussed the weather and the prospects for Ole Miss's success on the gridiron (both short topics), Dad mentioned that he had seen Jerry. Turns out Dad had needed a plumber. Jerry had finished his stint at Parchman, the state prison of Mississippi, and had learned a trade while there — plumbing.

"Son, tell me about Bogue Creek."

I suddenly became a twelve-year-old again as I told Dad the whole story. We both laughed, and I was grateful that the visit with Jerry had been short. There was much more that could have been told. It was strange how after all those years, I was still a bit embarrassed and ashamed that my misadventure had been revealed.

Imagine the woman at the well. All was revealed, and yet this man didn't speak words of condemnation, only loving acceptance. His eyes revealed grace and forgiveness. He offered living water that quenched every thirst of the soul. We all have our secrets. Some we wish could remain secret. But the one who knows them all loves us most. Thanks be to God. We are forgiven.

*Come and see a man who told me everything I have ever done! He cannot be the Messiah, can he?* — John 4:29

# Belonging

There is a man who lives on a mountain in Alabama. Shake Rag doesn't have any mountains, unless you count Chalk Bluff. Chalk Bluff is just that, a bluff that is as white as Mama Bea's freshly bleached sheets. Back when, the young folks would ride their mules over and have bonfires and roast hotdogs. Kids are too sophisticated for that today. There's not an app for that.

Anyway, this is a story about a man, and it starts when he starts, with his parents. His parents were a couple of young people who made a bad choice in life that resulted in a pregnancy. Sixty-plus years ago, this was a source of shame and humiliation for families. The local sheriff came and gathered up the young man, took him and the young woman to the local judge, and forced them to get married. It didn't last long, the marriage, that is. It was really just to give the soon-to-be-born son a name. The young couple divorced and went their separate ways. The father remarried and soon had children he was very proud of, but his firstborn remained a family secret. The "family secret" grew up, joined the army, went to jail for a period, and then moved onto a mountain and lived in the woods. No house, no plumbing, no electricity, just the woods.

The mountain man knew who his father was and kept a watchful eye on his secret family. During family reunions the mountain man would linger along the fringes of the woods, watching, just watching. It sounds a bit scary and strange to us, but it was hardly that. It was really more about a young man who wanted to belong. He could see his own face in the face of his dad and no doubt felt a connection that was powerful. Yet he remained on the fringe, just watching. Never being a part.

He eventually married, had two children, and built a one-room shelter for his family from scraps of lumber that he picked up here and there. He made a living from harvesting ginseng from the woods and selling it. He became well known in the little community nearest him. He was known to be trustworthy, despite his oddities. He once wanted to borrow $500 to buy a car. He walked into the nearest bank, told them what he wanted, and walked out with $500. No collateral, just his good reputation.

One day, one of his half-sisters learned about the family secret. She pondered what to do. She decided it was time to meet this mountain man who was her brother. She took a drive, turned down a road that led deep into the woods, passing "No Trespassing" signs all along the way. She was a bit nervous, wondering what kind of reception she would receive. She pulled up to what can only be described as a shack and got out. She was greeted by a rough-looking man dressed in overalls, no shirt, a beard down to his belly button, and a shotgun. But she didn't see any of that. What she saw was the face of her dad. "Hello, my name is...." He cut her off and said, "I know who you are." They hugged; he invited her in. Now she visits this brother on a regular basis. She has begun taking her daughter. They belong.

How many times have we stood on the fringes, wanting to belong? How many times have we overlooked those standing outside the circle of inclusion? What a tremendous gift of grace this sister offered when she reached out and gently pulled the "family secret" into the circle of welcoming love. We can do that. We can, with a little effort and just a bit of courage, reach out and include others. Jesus did: the woman at the well, Zacchaeus, the thief, the rich young ruler, Mary, the adulterous woman...me...you.

Mama Bea might say, "Come in the house."

God says, "This son, this daughter, was lost but now is found."

## Balancing...Life

Watching Zachary conquer problems can be a form of entertainment in our house. Some time ago, I told Zachary to clean up his many little messes throughout the house. Determined to make one trip, he began in the dining room and meandered through the kitchen, then the living room, and down the hall. All the way he was picking up balls and cars and clothes and everything else. It was quite amusing to see him attempt to balance all his stuff and make it to his room. He was determined. Each step, however, resulted in the loss of a car or some other item so that now there was a trail of items leading to his room. It was obvious that this was a multitrip task, but he was determined.

It was puzzling to me how he could have ever devised such a plan. Puzzling until a few days later when I stood on my front porch wondering how I could have devised my own foolish plan. Going to the grocery had resulted in many grocery bags, and there I stood on my front porch. With a plastic bag of groceries on each finger and a large bag of dog food balanced on my shoulder, I was certain I could get it all in one trip. That is, until I got to the porch and discovered the door was locked and my keys were still in my pocket. The neighbors must have gotten a good chuckle.

God must be amused with us also. We don't just balance bags or fill our arms with stuff; we fill our lives with such clutter and have the audacity to think that we can handle just one more thing. We cram it all in: family, friends, exercise, jobs, volunteer hours, yardwork, housework, ballgames — all of it. We don't see that along the way, we drop things. Sometimes it's just a missed doctor appointment; sometimes it's something important like a child's recital or lunch with a friend. Eventually, we all realize that we have to put something down or stand on the porch with dog food on our shoulders all night.

It seems to me that as much as God might be amused at us, God would be far more pleased for us to slow down. We don't have to do it all in one trip. Not if it means losing something important along the way.

# A Wild Rose

My mom used to say that Mama Bea could grow anything. Mom thought it was the dirt she used from the barnyard. I think it was Mama Bea. Besides the huge vegetable garden, her yard was full of flowers. I don't remember what she grew; I just know she grew a lot of it. There were some flowers that she identified as poppies to me one time. She said that they helped you sleep at night. I didn't ask any questions. She had the elusive green thumb that seems to have disappeared from the DNA chain after her. She once dropped a nail on the ground, and the following spring there was a hardware store in that very same spot. She was good.

Mama Bea enjoyed sharing her plants with others. I think she took great delight in digging up a plant, wrapping the root ball in a paper sack, and sending it off to another home. The house where I grew up was surrounded by plants and flowers that had migrated from Shake Rag to Grenada. Along the back fence there was a rosebush that had come from Mama Bea's. It must have been twenty feet long. Someone said it was a wild rose. Every spring it bloomed for about a week, and then it was done.

When Dad died, I dug up a piece of the bush and took it back to Waco. I planted it in a sunny spot, watered it, and waited…and waited…and waited. Nothing. Three years went by, and the bush not only did not bloom; it didn't grow, not even an inch. I guess being wild also means being stubborn. When we moved to Huntsville, I dug up the pitiful plant, threw it in a bucket, put it in the truck, and planted it some three months after moving into our new home. After just a few days, it began to perk up. It grew…and grew…and grew. I think it sent runners out at about the rate of a foot a day. Then in May, like it always did in Grenada and has ever since here in Huntsville, it began to put on buds, little bitsy buds that begin with a yellowish tint and then open to white blossoms. Today, right now, there are about 200 blossoms on the bush. They will showcase their beauty for about a week, and then they will be gone until next year.

The wild rose requires a lot of work for just a week's worth of enjoyment. I'll cut it back at least three times during the summer and will suffer the pricks of some wicked thorns. It will never be tamed. But it is worth it, at least for me. The bush begins calling to me with the first signs of spring each year. I'll peek out a window, watching for the first of those tiny buds to appear. They are reminders. They remind me of a childhood that is long since gone, along with my parents and my grandparents. They remind me of the good and the bad of growing up at 922 Franklin Street in Grenada, Mississippi. They remind me of my roots in Shake Rag and a farm that nourished many bodies and my soul.

"A wandering Aramean," the Hebrew grandfather begins as he recounts the story of his people (Deuteronomy 26:5). He remembers because it is important to remember, the good and the bad, the lean times and the times of abundance, the delicate blossoms and the wicked thorns. We remember because where we came from makes us who we are and what we will become. We remember because it is important to recall God's presence through all that life offers: the celebrations and the healing graces of pricks from life's wicked thorns. Despite our hard work, life will always be untamed, offering us a full slate of experiences. Thanks be to God for his faithfulness through all of it.

# Water Haul

On the farm in Shake Rag, there were two ponds. The pond by the house was the bait pond. Daddy Freeman had rigged a giant dipping net on the end of about a thirty-foot metal pipe. It pivoted on a post so that the weight was distributed and the net would not be so heavy, especially when it was wet. We would lower the net into the water, throw some cornbread out above the net, and in just a minute or two could raise the net, capturing plenty of minnows and goldfish for a day of fishing.

The other pond was further away from the house, out across the pasture. That's where the big fish were. Mama Bea liked to fish with the minnows; we big guys (all of eight years old) liked to fish with a rod and reel. It seemed the fish in this particular pond were fond of plastic purple worms. We would rig the hook so that the worm twirled in the water as it was reeled in. This seemed like a fair proposition for the fish. They could bite or not, then, if hooked, fight ferociously to escape, and they often did. I still remember a perfect cast of my line, landing my purple worm less than a foot from the bank when…WHAM. The worm was gone, and my line came whizzing back past my ear. It was the one that got away. My nephew, at the ripe ol' age of four, would hook a five-pound bass one day. His didn't get away.

A not-so-fair proposition for the fish was when we seined. A seine is a long net that would stretch from one bank to the other. It had floats on the top and lead weights on the bottom. On either end would be a pole that was used to pull the net through the water. This was always an exciting time because it usually meant a fish fry was coming, but better than that, I could get in the pond to help with the seine. I would follow along behind the seine, and if it got hung on a snag, I would free the net. Catching a snag was never good because it might tear the net, but it also gave the fish an opening to escape. It was great fun to finally pull the net up on the bank to see what the catch was like. You never knew because pulling the net through the water always made it feel full, even when it wasn't.

A good haul would include large bass and catfish. For us kids, a good haul included a turtle or two and a snake. We once caught a turtle that was so big it hissed at us while snapping at anything that moved. Every so often, the net would not be held to the bottom of the pond as it was pulled through, and all that would be in the net were a few tiny bream and moss. If the seine was pulled through the pond without holding the seine down again, the same thing would happen.

Daddy Freeman called it a "water haul." No matter how many times or how hard everybody worked, if done the same way, there would only be a water haul.

The disciples knew about water hauls. John tells us in his Gospel that the disciples had fished all night with nothing to show for it. A stranger on the shore tells them to cast their nets on the other side of the boat. This must have given them pause. "The other side is the same as this side," they must have thought. But there must have been something in the voice, something of the man's silhouette that got their attention because they did it. These professionals tried something new, as insane as it must have seemed to them. They probably didn't know our definition of insanity is doing the same thing over and over, all the while expecting different results. So they did it. They listened. They obeyed. WHAM! The catch was huge, and they realized what maybe they suspected but were afraid to accept. It was the Lord.

Listening can be hard work. Sometimes harder still is obeying, especially when it requires something new of us. Even small changes in life can be too hard and sometimes seemingly silly. If we take stock, though, and listen, maybe we realize that some changes are in order. Doing the same thing over and over, expecting something different, plodding along in our faith journey, and all we have to show for it is a water haul. How about being more attentive, more intentional, more willing to venture out and do something new? Let's listen to that voice that calls out and says, "Try the other side." It might work. And, well, that voice just might be the Lord's. If he appears to be a stranger to you, you definitely need to listen…and try something new.

# Turkeys and Thanksgiving

Thanksgiving today is far different than my childhood. Growing up we would gather up the casseroles and climb in the '62 Ford and head to Mama Bea's. If you have read much of my stuff, Mama Bea may seem as familiar to you as your own grandmother. Mama Bea, as you know, lived in Shake Rag, which was out from Okolona, which was down the road from Tupelo, which is where Elvis was born.

Mama Bea and Daddy Freeman raised a variety of animals on their farm. They had the usual cows and chickens, but they also had some unusual animals. They had peafowls. Peafowls are those beautiful birds that you usually see at zoos as they strut around with their million brilliantly colored "feather-eyes" staring back at you. They raised quail for a while. This was started one day when Daddy Freeman and I were walking across the pasture and came upon a quail's nest filled with little ones. He took them back and raised them to adults and pretty soon had quite a covey.

They also had turkeys, although they weren't around as much as the chickens or the guinea (funny-looking fowls from Africa). I never could decide if turkeys were smart or dumb. They wouldn't nest close to the house like the chickens would. They wandered off across the pasture and into the woods. If you wanted to know where they were nesting, you had to follow them. As soon as we would see a hen heading out, we would follow, eventually finding the nest. As I recall, Daddy Freeman would then go back at a time when the hen was off the nest and get the eggs. He would take the eggs and put them under a chicken that was setting (for you city folk that's what a hen does when she is incubating eggs). This was necessary because if the turkey eggs were left in the woods, they would be robbed by foxes or raccoons before they ever hatched. But Daddy Freeman wouldn't just take the turkey eggs; he would also leave behind fake eggs, something to fool the hen into thinking that all the eggs were there and the nest was undisturbed. Otherwise, off she would go to make a new nest. So the turkey was smart enough to hide her nest, but when it came to the eggs, not so much.

Now, I wouldn't want to compare people with turkeys entirely (although I have known a few turkeys in my life), but I do see a similarity. As we gathered around the table this year, there were many thanksgivings offered up for houses, prosperity, cars, jobs, football teams (not me), and a host of other pleasures that we surround ourselves with. No doubt, all blessings, but really aren't they more like those fake eggs in the turkey's nest? Don't they replace what is valuable in our thinking with false comforts and security? What really is most important? Family? Friends? It really is a much shorter list than we may think, if we stop to think. Let's give thanks to God for what is really important and not let others define what is important for us. We may or may not have full tables, but at the very least we'll have full hearts.

# Beagles

As my keyboard meandered its way through the woods of Shake Rag chasing turkeys, I was reminded that I hunted rabbits in those same woods. Armed with Daddy Freeman's single shot 20-gauge shotgun, I would call the dogs up to the house and then head for the woods. Daddy Freeman's dogs were service animals first, then pets. Mike was an English Setter that had been around since God had planted the grass. He was a pretty good bird dog, but what I liked most about Mike was his snake-hunting ability. Mike and Mama Bea shared an equitable amount of hatred for water moccasins. He and I would often just go snake hunting. He would spot a snake at the water's edge, grab it, and shake it until there was nothing left to shake. There is no telling how many times he was bitten. Then there was Mary and her clan. Mary was the queen beagle. She had a great nose and a distinctive yelp. You could always tell when they were on a rabbit. Often, she and the other beagles would go out hunting all night and make it home in time for breakfast, which was usually a pan of cornbread that Mama Bea had cooked the night before.

So off we would head into the woods. I would make my way to briar patch after briar patch, giving it a kick and a stomp. Eventually a rabbit would pop out, and the hunt would be on. Hunting rabbits with beagles is not like the pictures you see of dogs hunting foxes. Beagles tend to walk rather than run, relying on their noses rather than their eyes to follow the rabbit. Surprisingly, the rabbit isn't much faster. It does have that initial burst out of the briar patch. After all, a beagle's bite is worse than its bark, so it clears out pretty fast. But then, after a bit of distance, it will slow down, rest, hop a bit, rest some more. The rabbit will stay a safe distance out in front of the dogs. Funny thing about rabbits: they run in circles, big circles. Always. No one knows why since no one can speak rabbit. Some speculate that it is because they are just staying within the area they call home. They don't know what lies beyond, so why risk going there? Some think they are doubling back to confuse the dogs. Whichever, they run in circles.

The beagles never catch on to this. Noses to the ground, they'll trail right along behind that rabbit when what they should do is just sit and wait. If they would just pause long enough to take a look around, maybe they would spot the furry critter and get a clue. Nope. Noses to the ground, yelping, following, trailing, persistently, predictably, hunting. They run until they get tired or the hunter has, well, you know. Then they head home for a pan of cornbread.

Ever felt like you were running in circles? Are you going through life with nose to the ground, predictably doing what you always do? You might do it well, but it's the same ol', same ol'. We all do at some time or another. I suspect even my surgeon friend over in Mississippi looks down occasionally and thinks, "Same old gall bladder-ectomy." When that happens to me, it's time to not just pause and look around, but look up. Brother Lawrence, a monk in the seventeenth century saw God in the mundane. He said, "It is enough for me to pick up but a straw from the ground for the love of God." All we do, even chasing rabbits, is done for the kingdom and our Lord. Even much of what we do through the course of a week can make it seem like we are running in circles. Before we wear ourselves out, let's pause in those times, look up, and thank God that we are able to do, to be, to love, and to share — for others and, more importantly, for the Christ's sake.

*And whatever you do, in word or deed, do everything in the name of the Lord Jesus, giving thanks to God the Father through him.* — Colossians 3:17

## Christmas Sounds

When you picture the manger, what do you hear? Stop for a moment, imagine, and listen. This is what I hear. There is a gentle breeze blowing that whistles ever so gently. There is an occasional bleat of a sheep, a distant call of a mother to her child. "Aaron," she calls. Then there is the rustle of straw and an ever so faint coo of a baby. The mother hums a lullaby that her mother hummed to her. All this punctuated by silence. Holy silence.

Quite different from the sounds found at our house on this night. Tumbling down the stairs will be music that I find distasteful but apparently captures today's teenagers — something by singers called "Caesar" and "Three Days Grace." The names sound sort of biblical, I guess. Then there's that bouncing sound. That would be the five-year-old bouncing off the walls. In the guest bedroom behind a locked door, there is the rustle of wrapping paper. I'm not allowed in, and it's just as well. I'm content just listening. Eventually, all that will stop for a moment as we gather together to listen to the Christmas story being read. Then we are off to bed, and aside from the occasional "Is it morning yet?" there will be silence.

Silence is a gift. I know I crave it often. But even as I type these words, I am reminded that so are the sounds that fill my world. Loud music, sibling arguments, the soft sound of Jana's voice, race cars crashing down stairs, phones ringing with invitations to dinner or tennis — these are the sounds of my world, and they are the sounds of family and friends. They are all gifts to me, every day. Thanks be to God for each and every one.

# Christmas Laughter

Several years ago I was associate pastor in a church very similar to my current church of Weatherly Heights. We followed the liturgical calendar, supported women in ministry, believed strongly in missions, and shared a few other distinctives. We also had a Christmas Eve service. The service began at 11:00 P.M. every Christmas Eve and was a strange mix of formal and informal. The ministers wore robes, the organ played, we sang the familiar Christmas hymns, and we would light the Christ candle. In an effort to encourage young families, children were invited to come in their pajamas. It was a wonderful service.

One year during the service, we had entered into a most solemn time. It was an extended period of silence in which we prayed and reflected on the coming of Christ into the world. As I stood next to my pastor on the platform and pondered on the significance of the moment, I folded my arms across my chest. I was in deep, deep thought. Then, as if on cue, came a faint sound, a musical something. It came swirling around my head and began to gain momentum and volume. The sound was a tune, an electronic tune. It was "Here Comes Santa Claus." It could have been a cell phone today, but it wasn't. Its point of origin began to awaken within me a most terrifying thought. Could it be? It was. It was me! My new Christmas tie had a button in it, and when I had folded my arms, I unleashed its power. The coming of Christ had been upstaged by the coming of Santa. I tried to stop it. I grabbed the tie that had bunkered itself under my heavy robe. I found the button and pressed it. The tune started over. I pressed it again. It started over again. What do I do? I decided a dash to the U-Haul store might be appropriate but remembered it wouldn't be open for a couple more days. Maybe if I look at my pastor with a quizzical expression, the good folks in the congregation would think it was him. I looked over, and he wasn't smiling, so I ruled that out. I finally managed to grab the tie and shove the device under my arm and held it there. Now only a faint sound, somebody said amen, the organ began, and we began singing. Saved.

I've got to believe that at such times, God must certainly smile, even laugh at us and with us during such foibles. Seeing a young minister become glowing red enough to challenge Rudolph on the night of such importance must bring God a sense of pleasure in knowing that meaning well is enough when things go awry.

It also causes me to appreciate the gift of forgiveness. The pastor never said a critical word. The congregation chuckled about the experience, especially at

Christmastime in the years following. It really was a small thing. I've done much worse. But every time there have been those gracious souls who have smiled and forgiven. I've tried to do the same. There are many gifts that Santa brings this time of year, but none so great as the gift that came with the Child — the gift of forgiveness…of ourselves…and of others. Thanks be to God.

## The Mansion

The old house at Shake Rag burned down one day. You've read that in another story. That wasn't the house I remember. The house I remember was its replacement. A counter was added to split the kitchen from the dining table, so I guess with a little creative thinking it might have been considered a five-room house. There was nothing special about this rural farmhouse except that everything was special. The living room had three chairs and a couch. Two of the chairs were recliners that had been given to Mama Bea and Daddy Freeman as gifts from loving children. Daddy Freeman's was as hard as the concrete block he sat on outside to clean the fish. Mama Bea's was more suitable for her to rest in, which was seldom, except for the afternoon nap she took after putting the dinner dishes away, drinking a bottle of Coke, and watching *As the World Turns*.

At one time there was a giant fish bowl in the living room. The scar on my left leg leaves little to guess what happened to the bowl. There was a Pillsbury Doughboy and girl that were Christmas gifts, pictures of family, and a color TV. There was a coffee table too, although I don't remember anyone ever drinking coffee around it. That was done at the dining table, sometimes from a cup, sometimes from the saucer. There were two bedrooms. One bedroom was where guests slept when they came to visit. As I recall, the only ones who ever slept in that room were my parents and Uncle Fred and Aunt Linda. They came down from Coldwater, up near Memphis, every so often. It used to irritate Mama Bea just a bit that Aunt Linda slept past breakfast time. I don't think she ever complained, but her face, well, it told a different story.

The other bedroom was where Mama Bea, Daddy Freeman, and I slept. The room was big enough to have a double bed and a half bed. I always slept there, even when my long, skinny frame extended well beyond the bounds of the footboard. There was a fan in the room. The fan was an electric motor that Daddy Freeman had attached a car's engine fan to. Stick a finger in it, and you regretted it for a very long time. The small closet held the few clothes they had, which, by the way, were always starched and ironed. At the bottom of the closet were a couple rags that Tiny, their dog, slept on. I hated that dog. It would sit in Daddy Freeman's lap and growl at me.

In the hall were the shotgun and rifle. The stove was there. Not the oven, the stove. The stove was the house's heater. It was gas and sat there in the hall waiting patiently all summer until it would finally get its call in late fall. The telephone was in the hall. A useful tool, that telephone. When traveling home, we would ring it once and hang up. They knew their children had made it home safely without incurring any charges from Ma Bell. It also kept them informed about the Shake Rag gossip, particularly if you happened to pick up when the neighbor down the road was on the line.

Then there was the kitchen. A well-used oven, butter churn, and refrigerator resided there. Oh the magic that Mama Bea could perform. Made-from-scratch biscuits. Fried chicken. Apple jelly. Fried corn. I still crave each of those and much more. There was a chair there that Daddy Freeman always brought his socks and black leather shoes to in order to put them on. It must have been just the right height. In the drawer was a butcher knife. Most knives have a straight edge, but this one had an arch in the middle. It served as evidence of the thousands of ears of corn that Mama Bea had cut and scraped through the years. Just off the kitchen was a small room or large closet that housed the hundreds of jellies, jams, and vegetables that had been canned and preserved. There was a chest freezer and another refrigerator, which must have been the first Frigidaire ever made. There were other special things in the house, like the old radio that the three of us listened to gospel music every Sunday morning along with a little preaching. I guess it was their substitute for going to Mount Olive Baptist just down the road.

Jesus said he would prepare a place for us. I think I just described what I hope mine is like. I suspect that Mama Bea is happy if there is an oven, a bottle of Coke, and *As the World Turns* playing once a day. Daddy Freeman? He'll be happy where Mama Bea is. And that spiteful little dog. And Mom and Loretta and a host of brothers and sisters. A few cows would be a bonus, but not in the house. Well, I guess that is what we all want, really. To be with Jesus and family, that is. We'll all get there someday. For now, I'll cling to my memories of Shake Rag and work on creating new ones with Jana and the kids.

## Billy's Grand Adventure

Some of you may remember Billy Brown from the first story in this series. Billy was a TV repairman who lived in Shake Rag. His parents had lived there also and were buried in the Boone's Chapel Methodist Church cemetery, along with the rest of the Shake Rag community who had gone on to their reward. Billy had one arm but could carry a full thirty-two-inch, in-cabinet TV all by himself. He was also single and had a twinkle in his eye toward my sister Judy. Perhaps that's another story.

I went to visit Billy a couple weeks ago. The Sullivans were having a family reunion, and Mama Bea originated from that clan of Irish southerners. I decided to drive out to the Boone's Chapel cemetery, and that's where I visited with Billy Brown. He too had gone on to his great reward some years ago. There was his marker, right next to his mama and daddy. It was a nice marker, and his resting place was in the corner of the cemetery, just a few over from Mama Bea and Daddy Freeman.

Seeing Billy reminded me of a trip he once took on the Continental Trailways bus. Continental Trailways and Greyhound were the main contenders for transportation years ago. You could travel north and south on the Illinois Central Railroad, and some of the brave souls could fly. The bus, however, went in all directions. I suspect there were few Shake Rag citizens who rode the train. Even fewer flew, except for those who went to war in Europe and that conflict that flared up in Korea. So Billy wanted to take a trip on the bus. Trailways was offering a special at the time whereby an individual could buy a thirty-day ticket and travel anywhere in the continental United States. It didn't matter how many times you got off and on. You just had to be sure and time it so that you were home before the thirty days ran out.

Billy figured this would be a good and cheap way to see the country, so he began planning. Billy was a smart man. He didn't want to be bothered by luggage, so he packed a few clothes and necessities in boxes and shipped them ahead of him so they would be waiting at the bus terminal when he arrived. Billy left on his grand adventure. He kept an extra pair of unmentionables and socks with him, and if required, he would wash them in the sink at the terminal. He also carried all his meals with him. Now, don't think he had his mama's china and candelabra with him. Nor did it include the fine spread that was available at Mama Bea's table any Sunday. Billy feasted upon such southern delicacies as sardines, potted meat,

Vienna (pronounced Vy-enna) sausages, crackers, and Nabs. If you don't know, Nabs were those peanut butter and crackers packages that you usually acquired from a vending machine. I assume the name, which was common mostly in the South, was a derivation of the name "Nabisco," the maker and originator of such fine dining experiences. One can only imagine the aroma that wafted through the coach following the sound of tin being pulled back on those sardines.

When Billy arrived at a terminal, he would get his box of clothes and supplies. His dirty clothes and whatnot would be shipped back home, and he would be off to his next destination. Billy got off the bus at every destination. He would look around — around the terminal, that is — and get back on the bus with the satisfaction that he had visited that city. As far as I know, Billy never made it out of the terminals. When he arrived back in Shake Rag, Billy had seen the country, at least what views bus terminals had to offer.

That wasn't the only trip Billy planned for. As I said at the outset, Billy Brown was buried next to his mama and daddy at Boone's Chapel. He bought, paid for, and had his headstone placed well in advance of his demise. On occasion, Billy would go up to the cemetery to pay his respects. While he was there, he would lie down, fully stretched out, in front of his headstone. He would say, "I just want to make sure I fit." I suppose that is important to a man whose width and height were of equal dimensions. Needless to say, Billy Brown fit when the time came for him to board that final bus. Something tells me upon arrival to his destination that he wasn't satisfied with just visiting the terminal. I suspect that Saint Peter's greeting was enough enticement for him to venture on and see what grand adventure lay ahead.

We would all do well to take Billy's example of planning to heart. Christ said, "Who plans to build a tower without first counting the costs?" We need to examine our lives, measure them, and then set out to build a life that is pleasing to our Lord. We should seek to be examples to others. We should desire to be good disciples in service to our Lord and his people. Plan ahead. Also, plan to see more of the life of faith than just the terminals that you may pass through along the way. There is much more to our faith journey than what we learned as children and youth. Begin the grand adventure that we call prayer. Explore ways of praying that are old but new to you. Look beyond the terminal walls and see the world in which you live as a place that is in need of God's saving, healing grace. Find new avenues through the regular study of Scripture and by listening to the lives of the saints who have written volumes on finding your way along the journey. If you will do these things and a few others, you may just find your own grand adventure, with or without the Continental Trailways bus.

## It Was a Miracle, Too

Daddy Freeman and Mama Bea had daily rituals that began with the rising of the sun each day. Daddy Freeman was the first to clamor out of bed and begin his morning chores. If it was winter, he would fire up the heater so the house could warm a bit before Mama Bea got up. He then set about feeding the chickens their corn, the quail their mix, and the hogs that one day would be in the freezer or hanging in the smokehouse. Lastly, the dogs would get the leftover cornbread from the day before and whatever else wasn't suitable for the table any longer.

Mama Bea would soon be out of bed and making breakfast, which always included eggs with a distinct flavor that I have never found anywhere else. The yolks were a dark yellow and were no doubt the product of what the chickens fed on. We call them "free-range" chickens today. They called them breakfast or dinner. Soon the smell of home-ground sausage would wind its way around the house and cause me to get up. It seems city folks need more sleep than country folks. Add to this the scratch biscuits, homemade butter, fig preserves, and percolated coffee; well, let's just say that IHOP couldn't hold a candle to it.

Another part of Daddy Freeman's morning routine was milking the cow. Usually I only saw the milk when Daddy Freeman would bring it into the kitchen in a tin bucket. Bits of this and that would be floating in the milk, and Mama Bea would take a piece of cheesecloth and strain the milk into a gallon pickle jar and put it in the icebox. That's as close to pasteurization as that milk ever got.

On occasion I would get up early enough to follow Daddy Freeman out to the barn to milk. This was no Norman Rockwell barn. It was mostly a giant tin shed held together with baling wire and dirt dauber nests. A big gust of wind would one day take its toll, making way for a bigger and better tin barn. On one particular morning I was trailing Daddy Freeman step for step out to the barn, at least as step for step as any seven-year-old can follow an adult. When we entered the barn, we saw the milk cow lying down, which I had never seen before. Daddy Freeman quickly got me out of the barn. I was quite certain that she was about to give up the bovine ghost and Daddy Freeman was sparing me the ugly scene. I waited impatiently outside the barn — forever. Eventually, a grinning grandfather invited me in. I wasn't prepared for what I saw. When we arrived at the barn, there was only what appeared to be a sick milk cow. Now, right in front of me, were a recovering milk cow and a brand-new calf. My eyes betrayed my bewilderment as they were, no doubt, bigger than saucers. "Where did that come from?"

I blurted out. First there was one. Now there were two. It was a mystery. No, it was a miracle. Daddy Freeman didn't explain things to me that day. He left it to the hallways of elementary school for me to decipher the miracle of how births come about.

That day I witnessed only one of the daily miracles of farm life. From the first ray of light that finds its way into an egg that has a chick pecking its way to freedom to calves being born to a kernel of corn yielding its produce in the fall, it is all just the everyday occurrences of life on the farm. But each one is a miracle. The often-quoted words of Elizabeth Barrett Browning are true: "Earth's crammed with heaven, and every common bush afire with God; but only he who sees, takes off his shoes — the rest sit round it and pluck blackberries."

Miracles are as common in each of our lives as they were at Shake Rag. We find them in the mundane and in the explosive excitement of a baby being born. They are brought to us through messengers, doctors, grief counselors, and loving family and friends, even strangers at times. We only need to watch and listen. Simply pay attention and see God at work all around us, every day. If you do, your eyes may get as big as saucers, and you may find yourself exclaiming, "Where did that come from?" This time, you will know the answer.

# Epilogue

### *Monday, December 10, 2012*

#### Howard's Big Adventure

On Wednesday, December 5, Jana and I went to Kirklin Clinic in Birmingham for what we thought was preliminary work for an eventual liver transplant four or five years away. You may not know that I was diagnosed with cirrhosis about two years ago. The disease is genetic, meaning that my parents carried the defective gene and passed it on to me. When I was born, my genetics set off a timer that would result in my acquiring cirrhosis in my mid-fifties, thus the eventual need for a transplant.

After my blood work and CT scan, I met with the doctor who would head the transplant team. He gave me the news that I had a cancerous tumor on my liver that was 6.6 centimeters in size. Of course this was devastating. I went numb and at the same time into business mode, asking question after question. We learned that there is a treatment available that has had good success in shrinking the tumor. That is important. In order for me to be considered for a transplant at this point, the tumor must be reduced to five centimeters or less. It must then remain stable for six months.

The doctor also indicated that the CT scan seemed to indicate that the tumor had not invaded the liver. That was great news. If it had, options for treatment would be limited, and there would never be a transplant. I asked the doctor, given all he knows, what was his feeling about there being a good outcome, that is, a transplant and a cure. He confidently said that he was very optimistic. He threw out some percentages that would make a gambler in Vegas salivate. We were pleased.

The doctor took the initiative of arranging an unscheduled meeting with the surgeon that same day. The surgeon believed that the tumor had invaded the liver, so our roller coaster took a plummeting fall. He explained that my case would go before the tumor board the following Friday, December 7, and they would decide if I was a candidate for the preferred treatment.

Friday came with a phone call and good/bad news. There was consensus that the tumor had not invaded the liver and the preferred treatment was available. However, the nurse indicated that we would not be considered for a transplant because the tumor was 6.6 in size and the upper limit was 6.5! We were dumbfounded. How can that be possible? We wondered if our transplant doctor had not had accurate information. Fortunately, Jana had taken detailed notes. The doctor had said it was 6.6 and yet was very optimistic of our success. Then we remembered that he had spent a great deal of time talking about my young age, my overall health, my healthy diet and general care for myself. He said that would weigh heavily in my favor. We believe he is going to extend the boundaries for me because of those factors. I am still on track for an eventual transplant.

We think chemo and radiation will begin in a couple of weeks. We are waiting for another phone call with that information. The chemo's side effects will be minimal, with only flu-like symptoms for a few days. I will have two treatments, return in thirty days to check the size, hoping it has reduced significantly.

That is what we know as of today. I will try to stay current with information at this site. I will post on Facebook when there are updates. I hope you will refer to this as your source, as there have already been some misstatements by well-intentioned folks. This will also help ease the stress of telling my story over and over. I hope you understand. Jana and I appreciate your many encouraging words and prayers.

## *Monday, December 17, 2012*

### Howard's Big Adventure: The Latest

We have learned that I will go to Kirklin Clinic at UAB on January 2 for consultation concerning my chemo treatment. The next day I will be admitted at 6:30 A.M. for the procedure. I will stay overnight for observation and home on the 4th. The procedure will consist of running a catheter through an artery located in my hip area. The catheter will go all the way to the tumor, where they will release the chemo directly into/on the tumor. This treatment is highly successful. Because it is placed directly at the location of the tumor and does not go throughout my body as traditional chemo would, I will have minimal side effects. At the most, there will be flu-like symptoms for a few days. It is anticipated that this will be done twice within about a thirty-day interval. Radiation is likely to follow. There is a chance that the tumor will be completely killed with the first treatment, but it is not likely.

So many of you have been so kind in offers of help and the promise of prayer. There are individuals and churches from Texas to Indiana to the East Coast who are praying. It is good to have friends in these times. Jana and I are deeply grateful. We pray God's good gifts of grace and peace to each of you.

Howard

## Monday, February 11, 2013

### News from
### Howard's Big Adventure

"The results were ideal."

What does that mean?

"The tumor is dead."

Hearing those words was akin to discovering the elusive Fountain of Youth. It had been thirty days since the chemo had been administered directly into the tumor. By all medical accounts the hope was to shrink the cancer down by 1 centimeter, at minimum. There was almost an offhand comment made that someone once had the entire tumor destroyed with the procedure. They didn't dwell on that, but I did. Not to mention the hundreds of people around the country who had been praying. And it happened. Somehow between the chemo and the prayers, all that remained was the carcass of a creature that had invaded my body. Why it happened for me — and not one of the others who remains on our prayer list — is a mystery. I will never understand. I can only be grateful for my results and continue to pray for the others.

The next step now is to really kill the tumor. On February 25 I will return for a specialized radiation treatment to pummel what remains. Talk about beating a dead horse! They want to make absolutely certain that not a single cell remains. This particular tumor has a high incidence of returning. I will receive two or three treatments that week and be done, at least for that stage. Those treatments will carry me to March 1 and a ticking clock. I must go three months without a recurrence or a new tumor. Assuming that happens, a CT scan will verify it, and on June 4 I can officially be put on the transplant list. During those three months the radiation remains in my body and continues to work. That will help carry me right up to the day that I can be put on the list.

As a reminder, I have to have a transplant because my disease is genetically based. The day they remove my current liver, they will also remove the defective gene. The new organ will heal me completely. That has been our goal now for two years, but the cancer put me on a fast track for that to happen sooner than expected. Over the last three weeks I have been very sick because of some creepy crawly that is yet to be diagnosed. I have been assured that this plague is completely unrelated to my liver. I have lost a lot of weight because I am not getting the nourishment I need, despite having a good appetite. While it is nice to eat ice cream and cake in abundance, I would much rather be well. Hopefully my doctor will be able to help when I see him this week. We continue to thank God for your many prayers. We ask that you continue. Each stage is critical.

 Howard and Jana

www.ingramcontent.com/pod-product-compliance
Lightning Source LLC
Chambersburg PA
CBHW071220160426
43196CB00012B/2354